DID GOD
PLANT THE FORBIDDEN TREE?

BY
JOSHUA COLLINS

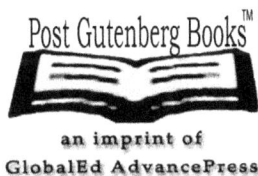

Post Gutenberg Books™

an imprint of
GlobalEd AdvancePress

DID GOD PLANT THE FORBIDDEN TREE?
  Copyright © 2010 by Joshua Collins

Library of Congress Control Number: 2010920302
  Collins, Joshua, 1980-
  Did God Plant The Forbidden Tree?
  ISBN 978-1-935434-42-9

  Subject Codes and Description:
  1. REL006060: Religion: Biblical Commentary – OT;
  2. REL.040010: Religion: Judaism-Rituals & Practice
  3. REL 006210: Religion: Biblical Studies – Old Testament

Cover design by Barton Green

Printed in the United States of America

Published by
Post-Gutenberg Books™
An imprint of
GlobalEdAdvancePRESS

TABLE OF CONTENTS

There are no alterations to any of the quotations (Biblical or otherwise) used within this text beyond what can be accomplished by a change in the character of the type (bold letters, italics, all capital letters, etc.).

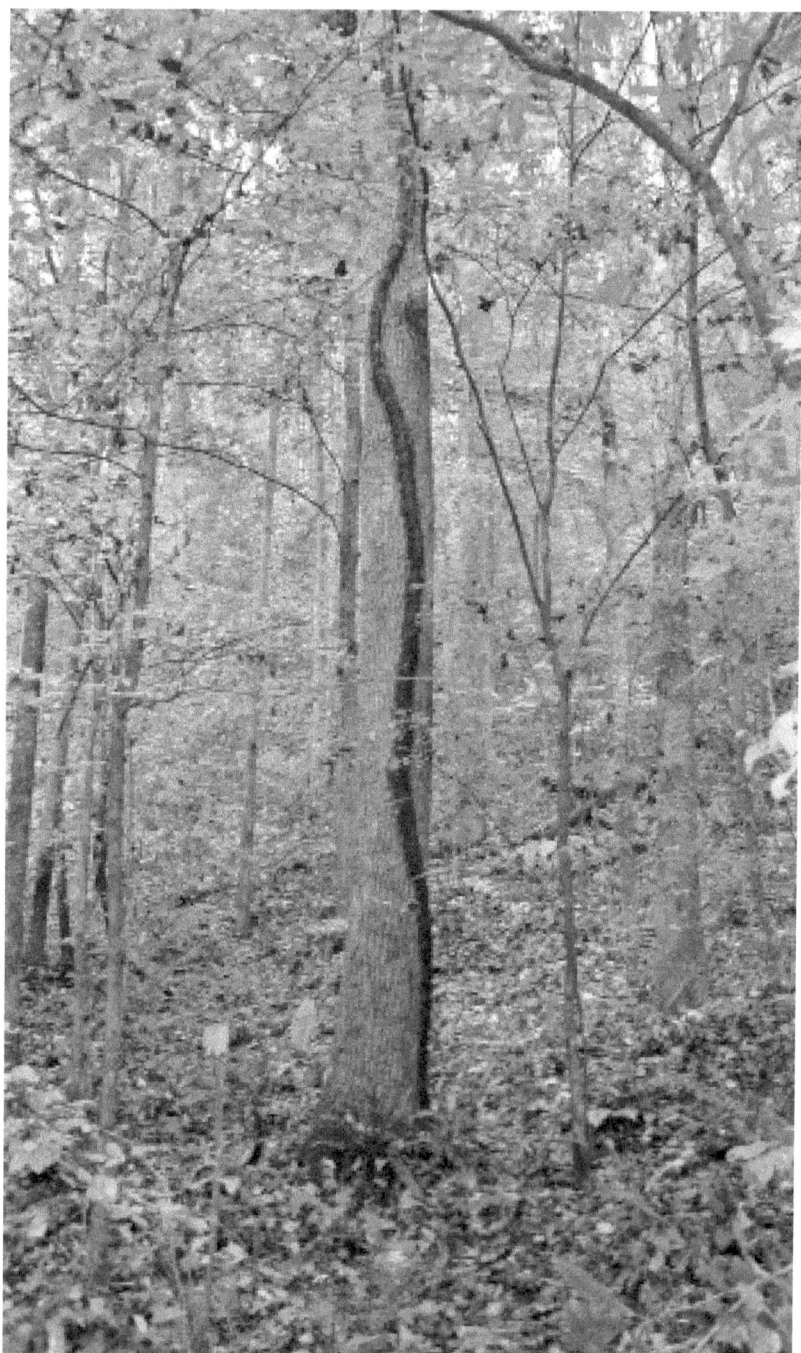

"For since the creation of the world God's invisible qualities — His eternal power and divine nature — have been clearly seen, being understood FROM WHAT HAS BEEN MADE, so that men are without excuse," (Romans 1:20).

"Open your mouth for the speechless, in the cause of all who are appointed to die," (Proverbs 31:8).

ACKNOWLEDGEMENTS

All credit belongs to the Lord God, for it is He Who has allowed me to research this topic and to write this book.

•••

This work was made possible through these servants of the Living God:

Dr. Leonard Heller and his wife Elizabeth Heller personally commissioned me to study this topic, though the book I have written was done secretly and was presented to them as a surprise. The Hellers are truly renaissance patrons, for they — out of their own pocket — funded my private study of God's Word. I am still baffled by their peculiar and selfless interest in my work, for a dollar-amount cannot be placed on the priceless gift of time. May God bless the Hellers for their patronage.

Rev. Dr. Robert Hale has given me over two years of his time in order to edit my work and to aid my studies by sharing his learning and his library with me. Dr. Hale's magnanimity cannot be estimated. I am honored by his endeavors to help me produce literature for the glory of Christ. He is beyond a rarity, and I hope I live long enough to attain his level of insight. May God bless Dr. Hale for his generosity.

Ms. Sharon Rehanek has provided me with an immensity of research materials, that were otherwise out of my grasp, by consistently purchasing numerous books for my library and my work. She has aided my Biblical research with unwavering support through careful edits of my manuscripts. I cannot thank her enough for her perpetual patience and kindness as I endeavor my utmost to leave a trail behind for others. I will never forget such generosity. May God bless Ms. Rehanek for her patient kindness.

Rev. Donna Kasik has continually encouraged my literary efforts for Christ, and she has offered her editing services whenever I have been in need of them. She has contributed vastly to my private library, and she has personally funded significant portions of my research. The faithful patron, Rev. Kasik, has my enduring gratitude, and neither of us will live long enough on the earth for me to repay her for her selfless and supportive deeds. May God bless Rev. Kasik for incessantly aiding me in my work.

(Edited by Rev. Donna Kasik, Ms. Sharon Rehanek, and Mrs. Elizabeth Heller)

FOREWORD

In my book, *The Knowledge of Good and Evil*, I wrote that God did not plant the forbidden tree. After this book was published, I discussed the subject at length with the erudite Oxford scholar, the Rev. Dr. Robert Hale, many times for more than a year. After considerable deliberation, I have found it necessary to expand on the point at hand. Surely God did not plant the forbidden tree. Let us consider the point of reference to which Christ connected His figure when He said,

> "Every plant which My Heavenly Father has not planted will be uprooted," (Matthew 15:13).

If the reader is under the assumption that God planted the forbidden tree, then it would be advantageous for the reader to ask, "Which plants did the Heavenly Father *not* plant?"

Throughout my conversations with Dr. Hale, he pointed out that the masses are almost uniformly unaware that Scripture is written in riddles. I was taken aback, but his words contextualized many of my lamentable disconnects when speaking with believers and non-believers alike; that is, when Dr. Hale pointed this matter out to me, it became apparent as to why I am often questioned (and sharply criticized) for "picking Scripture apart" as I do. The answer to why I "pick Scripture apart" is because I know of no other way in which to get to the bottom of a riddle. Of course, if Scripture is not understood to be a Book of riddles, then I guess my work might seem odd to those who read it; how much stranger my work must seem to those who do not read Scripture on a daily basis... It may prove beneficial to consider that the lack of "picking Scripture apart" has produced an abundance of beliefs in talking snakes, magic fruit, and the like.

Scripture is certainly sublime, spiritual discourse. Davidson's *Analytical Hebrew and Chaldee Lexicon* defines the Scriptural, feminine noun חידה as *enigma, proverb, parable*; hence *sublime, spiritual discourse*; this word also means *riddle* (as in Numbers 12:8) and it is from the root חוד *to tie* (as a knot); the Rev. S. C. Malan, D.D.'s work on the Book of *Proverbs* defines חידה *riddle* as a *twisted, tangled saying* (p. 19); consider a vine *interlacing* the branches of a tree, for vines were used illustratively to indicate riddles — thus we read of Christ, "The True Vine" (John 15:1) continually speaking in parables, riddles, enigmas, proverbs, dark sayings, etc. In Hebrew diction, a riddle is a verbal tangle, hence the root חוד *to tie*.

To an Ancient Hebrew-reader, the very fact that God spoke, combined with the fact that God is The King, would have indicated that God propounded riddles; for the verbs *to rule* and *to riddle* are both the Hebrew "משל," and this same root produces the word *oracle*. By strict diction, that the *Bible* is *sublime spiritual discourse* means that the *Bible* is a *riddle*, thus its description as the "oracles of God" governed by Scripture's own "principles" (Hebrews 5:12) and not human feelings, since "the heart of the sons of men is fully set in them to do evil," (Ecclesiastes 8:11). By strict diction, The *Ruler* is also The *Riddler*, hence, "It is the glory of God to CONCEAL a matter, but the glory of KINGS is to search out a matter," (Proverbs 25:2). Conceptions of regality entwined with parables form part of the linguistic basis concerning why Christ, the "King of Kings" (Revelation 19:16) and "The True Vine" (John 15:1) spoke in "parables" so often, for His parables (riddles, dark sayings, proverbs, similitudes, enigmas) are linguistically connected to His dominion, according to strict, Hebrew diction; consider when He says, "The KINGDOM of God IS LIKE..." Consider: "Now when the queen of Sheba heard of the fame of Solomon concerning the name of the Lord, she came to test him בחידות *with riddles*," (I Kings 10:1). When we recall that Christ is "King of Kings," and therefore Riddler of Riddlers, and when we reflect on the fact that Christ is also "The Word," (John 1:1), we might consider that The Word first had his Dictum scribed in Hebrew. Let us view an example of such *sublime spiritual discourse*; that is, let us view such Scriptural interlacing and *tying*, such Scriptural *riddling*.

The feminine noun באר *a well, a cistern*, is from the root באר *to expound, to explain* (as it is so employed in Habakkuk 2:2). Genesis 26:19 states that, "Also Isaac's servants dug in the valley, and found a well of *running water* there"; the English here states the meaning of the expression, but not the literal words that make up the expression itself (for a translator must choose one or the other according to the method of the translation). What we render "running water" from a well is the Hebrew מים חיים *living water*, thus, water that moves. We can therefore deduce that the concepts of "wells," "explanations," and "living water" are all related to each other, and we may consider that Christ, the *King, explained sublime spiritual discourse* concerning *living water* to a woman at a *well* in John 4; that this account was written in Greek does not nullify its strict Hebraic structure. Christ so spoke and so acted in deliberate accordance with the diction of the Hebrew Old Testament, which stands to reason when we consider the fact that He was the only One who fulfilled the entire Hebrew Torah. Of course, if one does not study the Torah deeply and makes the mistake of taking Christ's adversaries' words as accurate and truthful, then one will commit the blunder that assumes Christ somehow broke the Torah, the set of laws contained in ordinances by the hand of Moses.

Is not the New Testament the living targum of the Old Testament?

I seek to give glory to God for the intricate and wonderfully timeless Word He has provided under the specific contexts of the history and people to whom the *Bible* was first delivered. It may be beneficial to consider that God is often blamed for woes that cannot rightfully be attributed to Him when one ignores (or is unaware of) Scripture's elusive, yet unwaveringly precise, structure. I do not write in search of controversy, but being aware of my many personal shortcomings, blunders, and stinging failures, I write this work in pursuit of the truth in order that the King of Kings may be further glorified, and that we all may gain a greater understanding of His immeasurable love for us.

Sincerely,

Joshua Collins

INTRODUCTION

Even upon a casual reading of Scripture, it is evident that life and death are at continual odds with each other. It is also perceptible that the Almighty desires for us to live and not to die, for He does not take pleasure in the destruction of the wicked:

> "'But if a wicked man turns from all his sins which he has committed, keeps all My statutes, and does what is lawful and right, he shall surely live; he shall not die. None of the transgressions which he has committed shall be remembered against him; because of the righteousness which he has done, he shall live. Do I have any pleasure at all that the wicked should die?' says the Lord God, 'and not that he should turn from his ways and live?'" (Ezekiel 18:21-23).

Once death became a reality in the midst of God's creation, His love endured (and endures) as such:

> "I call heaven and earth as witnesses today against you, that I have set before you life and death, blessing and cursing; therefore choose life, that both you and your descendants may live; that you may love the Lord your God, that you may obey His voice, and that you may cling to Him, for He is your life and the length of your days; and that you may dwell in the land which the Lord swore to your fathers, to Abraham, Isaac, and Jacob, to give them," (Deuteronomy 30:19-20).

It is not questioned that a resounding quality of God is His desire for **life**. However, why is the aforementioned assertion not questioned when it is commonly believed that the "Living God" planted a tree that produced death in the very middle of the "garden in Eden" (Genesis 2:8)? How can it be claimed that the Living God planted a means of deathly temptation in the very abode that He Himself "planted" for humanity? — for it is written that God "...tempts no one," (James 1:13). Such a contradiction should be pursued to its bottom, lest we drift away into doubts concerning the character of the Living God. It should be observed that in the overt passages of Scripture regarding the Enemy, it is Satan's continual tactic to assist humanity in casting doubt upon the character of God. God is perfectly consistent; Satan is woefully contradictory. It should be common knowledge that, regarding the perfect justice and perfect mercy of God, when God administers punishment and grace, the punishment fits the crime perfectly and the grace fits the punishment perfectly; every, I repeat, every Scriptural account of God's punishment and mercy conforms to this principle impeccably. In other words, to claim that God's punishments (as related in Scripture) are random is to detract from our perception of His sense of justice; and to claim that His acts of mercy (as recorded in Scripture) are random is to detract from our perception of the perfection of His purposes. Let it be stated again: in Scripture, God's punishments fit crimes perfectly, and God's grace fits His punishments perfectly.

The creation "Days" contain many peculiarities (consider the fact that "Day Second" has no description of "good"). Let us focus on one peculiarity in particular: on Days "One," "Second," "Fourth," "Fifth," and "the Sixth," God Himself "said" and then God Himself did something; however, on "Day Third," God Himself "said," but it was the earth that did something.

On "Day One":   "...GOD SAID, 'Let there be light'; and there was light. And God saw the light, that it was good; and GOD DIVIDED the light from the darkness..." (Genesis 1:3-4).

On "Day Second":   "...GOD SAID, 'Let there be a firmament in the midst of the waters, and let it divide the waters from the waters.' Thus GOD MADE the firmament, and divided the waters which were under the firmament from the waters which were above the firmament; and it was so..." (Genesis 1:6-7).

On "Day Fourth":   "...GOD SAID, 'Let there be lights in the firmament of the heavens to divide the day from the night; and let them be for signs and seasons, and for days and years; and let them be for lights in the firmament of the heavens to give light on the earth'; and it was so. Then GOD MADE two great lights: the greater light to rule the day, and the lesser light to rule the night. He made the stars also..." (Genesis 1:14-16).

On "Day Fifth":   "...GOD SAID, 'Let the waters abound with an abundance of living creatures, and let birds fly above the earth across the face of the firmament of the heavens.' So GOD CREATED great sea creatures and every living thing that moves, with which the waters abounded, according to their kind, and every winged bird according to its kind. And God saw that it was good..." (Genesis 1:20-21).

On "Day the Sixth": "...GOD SAID, 'Let the earth bring forth the living creature according to its kind: cattle and creeping thing and beast of the earth, each according to its kind'; and it was so. And GOD MADE the beast of the earth according to its kind, cattle according to its kind, and everything that creeps on the earth according to its kind. And God saw that it was good. Then GOD SAID, 'Let Us make man in Our image, according to Our likeness; let them have dominion over the fish of the sea, over the birds of the air, and over the cattle, over all the earth and over every creeping thing that creeps on the earth.' So GOD CREATED man in His own image; in the image of God HE CREATED him; male and female HE CREATED them..." (Genesis 1:24-27).

It is evident that in each creation "Day," excepting "Day Third," God said something, and then God did something. "Day Third" is the "Day" that "seed" and "fruit" were set to be produced via the vegetation that appeared on that "Day." It must be remembered that it is the bride who is to bring forth fruit. The words ארץ *earth*, יבשה *dry ground*, and אדמה *ground* in the Hebrew creation account (Genesis 1-2) are all feminine, and the fact that man was "formed" from the עפר *dust* (masculine) of the אדמה *ground* (feminine) after a אד *stream* or *mist* (masculine) watered "the whole surface of the ground" would have indicated a resounding parallel to procreation to an ancient Hebrew; even in the period of the *Babylonian Talmud*, marriage was paralleled to a "fountain"

(*Babylonian Talmud*: "Ketubot"). That is, the description of masculine "stream" on the feminine "ground" is written just prior to the creation of Adam in a manner that is similar to a master potter forming a pot, for it is written that, "the Lord God יצר *formed (as a potter)* the man from the dust of the אדמה *ground...*" (Genesis 2:7). In the same way that the earth is watered for the purposes of fruit production, so man waters his wife for the purposes of "fruit" production, and the Hebrew idea of both pottery and procreation presented here in Genesis 2:7 is the same in Jeremiah 1:5 where God said, "Before I יצר *formed (as a potter)* you in the womb I knew you..." Such a method of communication may seem awkward to a Westerner today, but bear in mind the phrase "fruit of the womb" and it proves easier to comprehend the connection. The fertile union of water and land was commonly understood in parallel to human fertility in both the East and the West (see Pliny's *Natural History, Book V*).

Let us consider the "river" that flowed from Eden (Genesis 2:10). The name "Eden" comes from the same root as עדנה *anatomical femininity that is young enough to be capable of producing fruit*; in other words, when Sarah spoke of the female "delicate flesh" or "pleasure" (Genesis 18:12), she used the word under discussion, which is why the very next verse (Genesis 18:13) compares the viability of the womb to bearing a child.

> "Therefore Sarah laughed within herself, saying, 'After I have grown old, shall I have PLEASURE, my lord being old also?' And the Lord said to Abraham, "Why did Sarah laugh, saying, 'Shall I surely BEAR A CHILD, since I am old?'" (Genesis 18:12-13).

It seems that God quoted Sarah's thoughts behind her speech regarding "pleasure." In other words, when Sarah was quoted, God said that Sarah discussed "bearing a child" when our English Text simply states "pleasure"... not to say that the English is incorrect, but to point out that it is only English.

When we think of "Eden," it is imperative to think of a viable womb. The idea of a נהר *river* (masculine) that flowed out from "Eden" to "water the garden" (Genesis 2:10) relates the procreative union suitably and was once commonly understood even by children. Genesis 2:10 reads in its entirety: "Now a river went out of Eden to water the garden, and from there it parted and became four riverheads." Having already understood the water-and-ground union common to pottery, human procreation, and vegetable production, we should consider that this "river" became "four" riverheads. The word ארבע *four* comes from the root רבע which can mean "to lie with, carnally," i.e. *copulation* as it is so used in Leviticus 19:19; thus, when we reflect on the fact that "Day Fourth" was when the celestial lights were created, it stands to reason why those lights would have been used (ironically) to find the Holy Child, since no human copulation took place to produce His birth. A woman is called a "garden" in Song of Songs 4:12. Therefore, when the Torah says, "Now a *river* went out of *Eden* to water the *garden*, and from there it parted and became *four* riverheads," the prevailing concept is **life**, and humanity can understand such life through vegetable production and human procreation. Similarly, Christ said,

> "The kingdom of God is as if a man should scatter seed on the ground, and should sleep by night and rise by day, and the seed should sprout and grow, he himself does not know how. FOR THE EARTH YIELDS CROPS BY ITSELF: first the blade, then the head, after that the full grain in the head," (Mark 4:26-28).

Keeping in mind that it is the bride who is to bring forth the fruit, let us now reflect on "Day Third" of creation.

On "Day Third": "...GOD SAID, 'Let the earth bring forth grass, the herb that yields seed, and the fruit tree that yields fruit according to its kind, whose seed is in itself, on the earth'; and it was so. And THE EARTH BROUGHT FORTH grass, the herb that yields seed according to its kind, and the tree that yields fruit, whose seed is in itself according to its kind. And God saw that it was good..." (Genesis 1:11-12).

Notice that "Day Third" is unique amongst the other creation "Days" because, in it, God "said," but it was the "earth" that did something; the other creation "Days" overtly displayed God saying and God doing. Genesis 2:3 states,

"Then God blessed the seventh day and sanctified it, because in it He rested from all His work which God had created לעשות to make [i.e. created, so that it itself could produce, as David H. Stern's Complete Jewish Bible wisely translates]."

God is the "Husbandman" (John 15:1), that is, the Gardener. When a man waters his garden, fruit is produced. When a man waters his garden, his wife bears his child. Furthermore, when we consider יום Day שלישי Third in light of the "seed" and "fruit" in it, the Hebrew number ג three comes from the root גמל that can mean to ripen fruit and to wean a child.

When we reflect on the punishment administered to the woman who was named חוה Life after she sinned, it is plain that the original design of pregnancy and birth was to be lighter, swifter, and easier than what followed human sin. As such, it is necessary to consider the "river" that became "four riverheads" (Genesis 2:10) regarding the Eden narrative. The

Torah gives the names of the four heads, and the names are thematically deliberate and resoundingly descriptive:

> "Now a river went out of Eden to water the garden, and from there it parted and became four riverheads. The name of the first is פישון *Diffusion of Waters*; it is the one which skirts the whole land of חוילה *Bringing Forth, especially of a pregnant woman*, where there is gold. And the gold of that land is good; bdellium and the onyx stone are there. The name of the second river is גיחון *Belly, as the Source of the Fetus*; it is the one which goes around the whole land of כוש *The Womb** [note 1, p. 167]. The name of the third river is חדקל *Light, Swift*; it is the one which goes toward the east of אשור *Lifted Up, Exalted*. The fourth river is the פרת *Fruitful*," (Genesis 2:10-14).

After having recognized the shining procreative parallel within the creation account, we may observe the blatant description of how human birth was originally intended to be. That is, after the woman's *water broke*, she was to *bring forth* the baby from her *womb* in a *swift and light* manner and in the *exalted* joy of her *fruitfulness*. However, after the woman sinned, her punishment was this:

> "...I will greatly multiply your sorrow and your conception; in pain you shall bring forth children; your desire shall be for your husband, and he shall rule over you," (Genesis 3:16).

That is, after humanity fell, birth became extremely laborious. After human sin, again, AFTER HUMAN SIN, "...Adam called his wife's name חוה *Life*, because היתה *she became* the mother of all living," (Genesis 3:20). How can "Life" indicate something fallen? — we shall answer this question later; for now, let us understand that Adam's wife began under the dignified title of אשה *Woman*, but she ended under the name of חוה *Life*. Notice how the first time Christ referred to his mother in the Book of John (2:4), He referred to her by the pristine title of "Woman" that preceded the fallen title Adam gave his wife.

DISCLAIMER

Though Westerners may struggle with inductive parallelism, it should be constantly kept in mind that the *Bible* is decidedly not a Western Book. Accordingly, it is imperative that the reader understand the significance of the procreative descriptions highlighted within this book. In no way are such descriptions intended to highlight physical sensuality; rather, such descriptions are only highlighted to elucidate the consistent, weighted, and intense emphasis Scripture places upon **life** as opposed to death; be sure to read the notes at the conclusion of this book. That physical sensuality has been given to us by God as the means of reproduction does, in no way, mean that the sensuality is an end — for a means and an end are two different, though connected, entities. Therefore, I do not wish to be accused of being a sensualist by the fact that I am merely pointing out emphatic descriptions of **life** employed within Scripture; for it would be unfair to criticize a World War II historian for a violent inclination by the fact that he has merely chronicled the war itself.

Let us now attempt to untangle the tendrils of a buried history.

CHAPTER ONE

SEED

Scripture is deliberate and precise in its approach, and its precise deliberation is delivered with the utmost terseness. Let us keep this maxim in mind:

> "Every word of God is pure; He is a shield to those who put their trust in Him. Do not add to His words; lest He reprove you, and you be found a liar," (Proverbs 30:5-6).

When Scripture states something, it is imperative that we add nothing to what has been stated, otherwise we will fall short of reaching the truth of a matter. Assumption often leads to fault. For instance, let us examine the commandment given to Adam by God:

> "And the Lord God commanded the man, saying, 'Of EVERY TREE of the garden you may freely eat; but of the Tree of the Knowledge of Good and Evil you shall not eat, for in the day that you eat of it you shall surely die,'" (Genesis 2:16-17).

The prohibition above was delivered prior to the creation of Adam's wife, who was named **Life** ("Eve") after she was "deceived and fell into transgression" (I Timothy 2:14); she was not named **Life** before she transgressed. In order for her to have received God's prohibition, she must have received it secondly (from God) or second-hand (from Adam) since she was created after God commanded Adam not to eat of the forbidden tree (that is, unless we take "Adam" in the sense of Genesis 5:2, which seems doubtful in light of Genesis 2:18 and the employment of the article in Genesis 2:16 as opposed to the lack of the article in Genesis 5:2); whichever way, the commandment that God gave was not the same as what the woman recounted to the so-called "serpent" of Genesis 3, for she said,

> "...We may eat THE FRUIT of the trees of the garden; but OF THE FRUIT OF THE TREE which is IN THE MIDST of the garden, God has said, 'You shall not eat it, nor shall you TOUCH it, LEST you die.'"

Disregarding English translations, the woman said that God forbade "פרי *fruit...*" when He did not. God forbade humanity from eating "of the Tree of the Knowledge of Good and Evil"; God mentioned nothing of forbidden "fruit..." Throughout the entirety of the woman's discourse with the "serpent," the "serpent" never mentioned forbidden fruit. When Adam was questioned by God regarding human sin, Adam mentioned nothing about forbidden fruit. The prohibition was against the "Tree of the Knowledge of Good and Evil" with respect to consumption; the prohibition was not against only a portion of this tree.

The woman said that God forbade humanity from "touching" the Tree of the Knowledge of Good and Evil when He did not. God prohibited nothing from being touched.

The woman said that God gave a condition when she claimed that He said, "lest you die," when He did not. God pronounced nothing conditional. God specifically said, "...for in the day that you eat of it you shall surely die"; He pronounced a judgment, not a condition.

There were only two trees that were given proper names in the Eden Narrative, and God was specific as to which tree was prohibited. That is, God prohibited a tree by name when He said, "...but of the Tree of the Knowledge of Good and Evil you shall not eat..." and we may notice that the woman said that God forbade "the FRUIT OF THE TREE which is in the midst of the garden..."; in other words, the woman did not name the forbidden tree; she only gave the location of it. The cryptic difficulty of her statement is that Genesis 2:9 states that the Tree of Life was in the middle of the garden, and we may therefore gather that both trees were in the garden's center, at least eventually. A clue to why the woman did not name the forbidden tree, but rather said, "the fruit of the tree," is because "the fruit of the tree" is the literal, word-for-word, English rendering of the Ancient Hebrew expression denoting "wine unmixed with water," that is, wine that was not to be consumed.

Even seemingly slight deviations from the Word of God are disastrous. The fact of the matter is that the woman did not faithfully relay God's message. Furthermore, the fact that she was even dealing with the Enemy reveals that it was Adam who first sinned. Before the woman was even "built" (וייבן) in Genesis 2:22, Adam was placed in the garden לעבדה *to cultivate her* ולשמרה *and to guard her* (Genesis 2:15). The fact that the garden needed to be guarded indicates that there was some present threat. Scripture calls a woman a גן *garden* (Song of Songs 4:12), and we see that Adam did not guard the garden by the fact that the "serpent" was inside of it, and by the fact that Adam let his wife duel with the Enemy. Adam was specifically commissioned to guard, and he did not, which indicates why God did not give a condition based on humanity's actions, but rather, God pronounced a judgment according to humanity's actions (or lack thereof) — for Adam did not guard the garden; hence, "in the day you eat from it, you shall surely die," (Genesis 2:17).

In light of words like "garden" and "cultivate," let us keep in mind that the people to whom the *Bible* was first delivered were largely agricultural, and let us observe Day Third of Creation in order to examine what is specifically qualified according to what God said and what the earth brought forth:

> "Then God said, 'Let the earth bring forth grass, the herb that YIELDS SEED, and the fruit tree that yields fruit according to its kind, WHOSE SEED IS IN ITSELF, on the earth'; and it was so. And the earth brought forth grass, the herb that YIELDS SEED according to its kind, and the tree that yields fruit, WHOSE SEED IS IN ITSELF according to its kind. And God saw that it was good," (Genesis 1:11-12).

According to what God "said" and what the earth "brought forth," we may notice the deliberate emphasis placed upon זרע *seed*. All of which God commanded the earth to yield on Day Third contained seed. We may note these natural facts: (1) fruit, or produce, provides sustentation, but it is the seed that encapsulates perpetuity; (2) perpetuity promises life; without seed, there is no perpetuity and no multiplication (for seed will be produced even if plants are propagated by cuttings). Such facets of nature help explain much regarding the title of the "Living God" (Deuteronomy 5:26; Joshua 3:10; I Samuel 17:26 & 36; II Kings 19:4 & 16; Psalm 42:2; 84:2; Isaiah 37:4 & 17; Jeremiah 10:10; 23:36; Daniel 6:20 & 26; Hosea 1:10; Matthew 26:63; Acts 14:15; Romans 9:26; II Corinthians 3:3; 6:16; I Thessalonians 1:9; I Timothy 3:15; 4:10; Hebrews 3:12; 9:14; 12:22; Revelation 7:2) with regard to God's "heirs" (Romans 8:17). As such, we notice the emphasis placed upon life, as opposed to death, God as opposed to Satan; observe the contrast of "dead works" to the "Living God" in Hebrews 9:14. Consider the Living God as opposed to "the one who has the power of death, that is, the devil," (Hebrews 2:14). When God pronounced judgment in Genesis 3, He promised and prophesied redemption through an Heir, that is, זרע *Seed*, (Genesis 3:15; Galatians 3:16). In the fallen state of things, the perpetuity of natural life is impossible without seed.

When we observe the emphasis thrust upon seed, particularly as conveyed by Genesis 1:11-12, it is important to remember that when words denoting offspring, child, children, progeny, etc. are employed in the English Text, they are, sometimes, but a translation of the Hebrew word for "seed" used in Genesis 1:11-12 (for example: Genesis 13:16, 15:3; 16:10, etc.); let us consider one such example. In Genesis 16:10, the angel of the Lord said to Hagar, "I will multiply thy seed exceedingly, that it shall not be numbered for multitude"; of course, the "seed" in this passage refers to her family line, her progeny; it is the same word used for the "seed" discussed on Day Third of Creation (Genesis 1:11-12). As such, we understand that where seed becomes fruitful, there is life; "...God is not the God of the dead, but of the living," (Matthew 22:32). "Seed" and "heir" are understood as related terms.

When considering the pristine Creation, before any disease or strange mutation occurred, we must rule out certain factors. Seedless grapes (that is, grapes whose seeds do not develop a proper, hard coat) have arisen in fallen nature due to mutation, and natural mutation occurs in fallen nature commonly, as is true with human and animal bodies. Since physical malady in humans cannot be thought of as original to God's prototypical design because it would nullify His judgment regarding "death," the same must be true of other injurious mutations, for some vegetable mutations are non-viable and even lethal (and God's design was for life, not death). When we consider lethal mutations, harmful manipulations, etc., we may regard vegetation in the fallen state of things. Furthermore, even when propagating by cuttings, a plant that is not the product of human interference will produce seed as its parent produced seed. Grasses and daylilies can reproduce by stolons. However, we must keep in mind that the *Bible* is not to explain science, but rather science is set to explain the *Bible* (Romans 1:20).

The Text says that the vegetation that God commanded the earth to yield was "good," (Genesis 1:12); it does not say that the vegetation He made was both "good and evil." If one adopts the stance that God planted the Tree of the Knowledge of Good and Evil, then one will have to state that God was responsible for vegetation that was both good and evil — which then produces a contradiction. The "seed" God commanded the earth to yield was "good." All vegetation that God caused the earth to bear on Day Third of Creation contained "seed." Every tree that God commanded the earth to bring forth on Day Third contained seed in its fruit. God gave no prohibition against "fruit." Regardless of English translations, the only "fruit" that God Himself mentioned, regarding humanity between Genesis 1 and Genesis 3, is the "fruit" that humanity was to produce by procreation (Genesis 1:28) and the "fruit" that humans were allowed to eat (Genesis 1:29). God said nothing about forbidden "fruit." That the woman, the bride who was to bring forth fruit, was the only one who mentioned forbidden "fruit" illustrates how

> "...one is tempted by ONE'S OWN DESIRE, being lured and enticed by it; then, when that desire has CONCEIVED, it gives birth to sin, and that sin, when it is fully grown, GIVES BIRTH to DEATH," (James 1:14-15).

CHAPTER TWO

FRUIT

Scripture blatantly parallels the "seed" within the fruit of vegetation to the "seed" within the fruit of humanity, for, in essence, both entities function similarly. Accordingly, God's first command to humanity was to

> "...Be FRUITFUL and multiply; fill the earth and subdue it; have dominion over the fish of the sea, over the birds of the air, and over every living thing that moves on the earth," (Genesis 1:28).

By nature, fruit has seed in it, and such seed, when sown and nourished properly, causes multiplication. Like the word "seed," the word פרי *fruit* is applied, by Scripture, to both the productions of vegetable and animate life.

> "And He will love you and bless you and multiply you; He will also bless the FRUIT OF YOUR WOMB and the FRUIT OF YOUR LAND, your grain and your new wine and your oil, the increase of your cattle and the offspring of your flock, in the land of which He swore to your fathers to give you," (Deuteronomy 7:13).

> "Blessed shall be the *fruit* OF YOUR BODY, the *produce* OF YOUR GROUND and the *increase* OF YOUR HERDS, the increase of your cattle and the offspring of your flocks," (Deuteronomy 28:4; the English words *fruit*,

produce, and *increase*, are all the same Hebrew word
פרי *fruit*).

Recognizing that "seed" indicates "descendant(s)," and that
"fruit" indicates the same, we may understand what Fruit was
indicated when it was written,

> "Then she spoke out with a loud voice and said,
> 'Blessed are you among women, and blessed is the
> FRUIT OF YOUR WOMB! But why is this granted to me,
> that the mother of my Lord should come to me?'"
> (Luke 1:42-43).

The "Fruit" of Mary's womb is, of course, Christ, Who is the
"Seed" discussed in Galatians 3:16. The usage of "seed"
and "fruit" as representative words for humanity is a readily
understood method of Biblical communication. Reflecting
back upon Day Third of Creation, we can observe that the
nature of the vegetation that God commanded the earth to
bring forth was markedly seed-bearing, and that, specifically,
the trees that can be attributed to Him had seed in their
fruit:

> "Then God said, 'Let the earth bring forth grass, the
> herb that yields seed, and the fruit tree that yields
> fruit according to its kind, whose seed is in itself, on
> the earth"; and it was so. And the earth brought forth
> grass, the herb that yields seed according to its kind,
> and the tree THAT YIELDS FRUIT, WHOSE SEED IS IN
> ITSELF according to its kind. And God saw that it was
> good," (Genesis 1:11-12).

It is therefore evident that a deliberately marked characteristic
of the "fruit" that was yielded by the trees that can be
attributed to God was that such fruit housed seed. In other
words, seedless fruit had no part in God's command regarding
fruit-trees on Day Third of Creation; the fruit-trees that can be

attributed to God on Day Third were all seed-bearing, as is true of the natural order of things. We have already seen that both "seed" and "fruit" are used to illustrate people (and therefore progeny), and we have already noticed that the only "fruit" under the discussion of God's creation was seed-bearing fruit. As such, let us observe what God allowed people to eat:

> "And God said, 'See, I have given you EVERY herb that yields seed which is on the face of ALL THE EARTH, and EVERY tree whose fruit yields seed; to you it shall be for food. Also, to every beast of the earth, to every bird of the air, and to everything that creeps on the earth, in which there is life, I have given every green herb for food'; and it was so," (Genesis 1:29-30).

The superlatives ("every" and "all,") eliminate many outside factors. Respecting herbs, humanity was not given "some" herbs that yield seed; humanity was given "every" herb "that yields seed." Humanity was not given every herb that yields seed in certain geographical locations; humanity was given "every herb" that yields seed on the face of "all the earth." With respect to herbs, the herbs humanity could eat were seed-bearing, and of these seed-bearing herbs, humanity could eat of "every" one of them on the face of "all the earth." Therefore, if we should consider restriction, then the only "herbs" that could not be eaten would have been seedless herbs no matter where they existed, since "every" seed-bearing herb was given to man for consumption on the face of "all the earth" — but we have already seen that all of the herbs that can be attributed to God on Day Third of Creation were seed-bearing. With respect to herbs, since only seed-bearing herbs were given to humanity for food, and since God was responsible only for herbs that were seed-bearing, herbs that were not seed-bearing cannot be attributed to God.

Again, the superlatives ("every" and "all,") eliminate many outside factors. Respecting fruit-trees, humanity was not to eat "some" of the trees whose fruit yielded seed; humanity was given "every" tree whose fruit yields seed. Humanity was not given "every" tree for food; humanity was given "every" tree whose fruit "yields seed." Therefore, if we should consider restriction, then (having already noticed the established parameters) the only "trees" that could not be eaten would have been trees whose fruit was seedless — but we have already seen that all of the trees that can be attributed to God on Day Third of Creation had seed-bearing fruit. With respect to trees, since only trees that had seed-bearing fruit were given to humanity for food, and since God was only responsible for trees that had seed-bearing fruit, then any tree that did not have seed-bearing fruit cannot be attributed to God.

The Name אלהים *Elohim*, when used as a proper noun to designate God specifically, is plural, though it describes the One and only Deity. Ecclesiastes 12:1 warns us to "...remember בוראיך *your Creators*..." which agrees with the number of the Name "Elohim." Shall we assume more than one Creator? — certainly not. That certain references to God are plural in number explains the idiom conveyed by the language in which they were written, for He is uniformly manifold, hence His many Titles and His Three Personages. Accordingly, we must rule out any other "creator" when concerning ourselves with the aforementioned potential restrictions regarding seedless plants and the like. At the same time, to assume that "every" tree in existence is a direct result of the initial creation is a mistake when such is not even true when we buy produce at the grocery store. We may reflect on the Word of God when He said, "Every plant which My heavenly Father has not planted will be uprooted," (Matthew 15:13).

That which is created is distinct from that which is made from the creation, for we make many things that are not direct products of the natural order. Despite English translations, the Hebrew Scriptures do not say that "...He had rested from all His work which God created *and made*," (Genesis 2:3) but rather "which God created *to make*," that is, *to continue the production process.* However, on top of the capability to reproduce, entities can be made through the manipulation of things already in existence. People make vehicles; God created metal. People make houses; God created wood. People make sculptures; God created stone.

With respect to plants, that which is created is distinct from that which is planted, for we plant many things today that are not direct products of the natural order. Let us consider the fact that many of us eat seedless grapes on a regular basis; however, to assume that untouched and untainted nature would normally produce seedless grapevines is a faulty assumption. The seedless fruit we buy at the grocery store is a direct result of man's manipulation of nature, for nature normally produces seed-bearing fruit, not sterile fruit. Various hybridization practices cause sterility and barrenness. Natural grapes have seed in their fruit. God is responsible for seed-bearing vegetation, and the aim of this commandment is evident: "...You shall not sow your field with mixed seed..." (Leviticus 19:19); mixing two unlike things can yield seedless (and even lethal) produce, and the reader may understand that the thrust of this Torah law is not so much on biochemistry, husbandry, or farming, but on the concept of uniting two unlike entities against the design of nature. There is nothing more unlike than good and evil, for good and evil are direct opposites; the mingling of the two opposites produces unfruitfulness; consider the "unfruitful works of darkness" (Ephesians 5:11) in contrast to "...bearing fruit in every good work, growing in the *knowledge* of God," (Colossians 1:10).

The word "knowledge," as in the Tree of the *Knowledge* of Good and Evil, is דעת which comes from the root ידע *to know* (literally, *he knew*); this root is sometimes employed to signify *copulation*, as in, "Now the man [Adam] *knew* his wife Eve, and she conceived..." (Genesis 4:1). Of course, Adam's "knowledge" was his *union* with his wife. Therefore, the forbidden tree was the

> tree of the *knowledge* of GOOD AND EVIL,
>
> a tree of the *union* of UNLIKE ENTITIES...

for God separated light from darkness on Day *One* of Creation. The word אחד can be pronounced to produce the words *one* (Genesis 1:5) and *to unite* (Ezekiel 21:21), so we can see why "light" was, ironically, *divided* from "darkness" on Day *One* [The Day of *Union*]... for "light" was "good" (Genesis 1:4) and death was not. Regarding the Tree of the *Knowledge* [*Union*] of Good and Evil, we may understand that the forbidden tree was a product of the *union*... the marriage... the binding together... the mixture, that is, the *knowledge* of unlike entities... II Corinthians 6:14-18 commands:

> "Do not be unequally
>
> *yoked* TOGETHER with UNBELIEVERS. For what
>
> *fellowship* has RIGHTEOUSNESS with LAWLESSNESS? And what
>
> *communion* has LIGHT with DARKNESS? And what
>
> *accord* has CHRIST with SATAN? Or what
>
> *commonality* has a BELIEVER with an UNBELIEVER? And what
>
> *agreement* has THE TEMPLE OF GOD with IDOLS?

For you are the temple of the living God. As God has said: 'I will dwell in them and walk among them. I will be their God, and they shall be My people.' Therefore, 'Come out from among them and BE SEPARATE, says the Lord. Do not touch what is unclean, and I will receive you.' 'I will be a Father to you, and you shall be My sons and daughters, says the Lord Almighty.'"

Note that the quoted command, "Do not touch what is unclean" in II Corinthians 6:17 (Isaiah 52:11), seems to indicate that the woman's idea of not "touching" the forbidden tree (Genesis 3:3) may have expressed her knowledge that the tree of the union of unlike entities was, by nature, unclean... for the passage that immediately follows (II Corinthians 7:1) states, "...dear friends, let us purify ourselves from everything that contaminates body and spirit, perfecting holiness out of reverence for God."

Since "every" tree that can be attributed to God produced fruit that contained seed, and since "every" one of these trees was given to humanity for food, then the fact that God forbade a certain tree means that that tree could not have contained seed in its fruit, and this fact aligns seamlessly with the theme of the Fall of Man when we consider the mixture or union of unlike entities. It is therefore evident that the only "fruit" that was forbidden must have been seedless; if such fruit was seedless, then it cannot be attributed to God, especially when these facts are considered in accordance with God's allowance for humanity's sustentation in Genesis 1:29:

"And God said, 'See, I have given you EVERY herb THAT YIELDS SEED which is on the face of ALL THE EARTH, and EVERY tree whose FRUIT YIELDS SEED; to you it shall be for food."

That God created metal does not mean that God created cars; how much more true is this fact when dealing with abuses? There cannot be an abuse unless there is first a use. There cannot be an anti-anything unless there is first a thing. To state that God created abuse by the fact that He created use, or to state that God created an anti-something by the fact that He created something, is surely a fallacy, if not blasphemy; for to reason as such would be to say that God created fornication, adultery, pornography, prostitution, pedophilia, bestiality, homosexuality, and the permitted and applauded putridity glamorized on glowing screens by the fact that He created human sexuality — which is, of course, illogical and utterly blasphemous!

"Fruit" and "progeny" are understood as related terms. The Text says that the vegetation that can be attributed to God on Day Third of Creation was "good," (Genesis 1:12); it does not say that the vegetation that can be attributed to God on Day Third of Creation was both "good and evil." If one adopts the stance that God planted the Tree of the Knowledge of Good and Evil, then one will have to state that God was responsible for vegetation that was good and evil, and such a statement produces a contradiction. The fruit that can be attributed to God on Day Third of Creation was "good" and had "seed." As Scripture is so structured, God could not have been responsible for seedless fruit. Seedless, that is, sterile plants are the result of the unclean mixture of unlike entities; good and evil are the most unlike entities in the universe, hence the "Tree of the Knowledge of Good and Evil," the tree of the unholy unification that lead to sterility, barrenness, and ruination. God commanded fruitfulness (Genesis 1:28). God tempts no one (James 1:13). Therefore, God could not have planted the forbidden tree.

CHAPTER THREE

TREES

People are often compared to trees in Scripture (Judges 9:8-11; Psalms 1:3; 37:35; 92:19; Song of Songs 7:8, Daniel 4, Mark 8:22-25, etc.). Man is sometimes compared to an olive tree (compare Romans 11 to the imagery of Zechariah 4), hence Christ's statement: "You are the light of the world..." (Matthew 5:14), for the oil used for their lamps came from olives.

It is also worthwhile to note that the Hebrew Scriptures employ the word עֵץ *tree* to denote *the vine-tree* (עֵץ־הַגֶּפֶן i.e. a *vine*) in Ezekiel 15, which stands to reason when considering the similarity of a vine's wood, branches, etc. to what English-speakers call a "tree." Therefore, when reading the word עֵץ *tree*, it is necessary to understand whether or not a "tree" (as we call it) or a "vine" (that the Hebrew Scriptures call a "tree" or a "vine-tree") is being discussed. Context is the key. It was a common practice among the people in the time-frame and geographical proximity of the Scriptures to train grape-vines onto fruit-trees (consult the *Babylonian Talmud's* "Berakhot"), for fruit-trees served as trellises. Hence, the situation of a vine that coiled about a tree was understood as a situation of "two trees" that stood in one place. Furthermore, when considering "trees" and "vines," we also have to distinguish whether or not these forms of vegetation are trained or wild. Therefore, regarding trees, where the word עֵץ is employed, it is necessary to determine if a trained *tree*, a wild *tree*, a trained *vine*, or a wild *vine* is being discussed; this same word can also mean *wood* (Exodus 7:19), *timber* (Exodus 31:5), *stalks* (Joshua 2:6), a *staff* (I Samuel 17:7), a *stick* (Ezekiel 37:16), *stocks* (Hosea 4:12), and *gallows* (Esther 5:14); furthermore, this word "tree" can be singular or plural. Consider how this one word can mean both *a gallows* and *a vine*, like *a vine* on a trellis, like the *True Vine* (John 15:1) on the cross.

Scripture only gives proper names to two trees in all of the Creation account in what we now call the first three chapters of Genesis: (1) The Tree of Life, and (2) The Tree of the Knowledge of Good and Evil. Genesis 2:9 tells us that the Tree of Life was in the middle of the garden (in Eden); once the Sacred Text ceases from using the proper names of these two trees, Genesis 3:3 illustrates the fact that the Tree of the Knowledge of Good and Evil (the forbidden tree) was also in the middle of the garden. However, if the two central trees were both "trees" as we define trees in English, then the true "midst" of the garden would have been between the Tree of Life and the Tree of the Knowledge of Good and Evil. Yet, when the woman spoke in Genesis 3:3, "the tree" to which she referred (but did not name, i.e. the forbidden tree) was in the "middle" of the garden, and this statement makes sense when we regard what Scripture calls a "vine-tree" in terms of understanding the "Tree of the Knowledge of Good and Evil," i.e. the forbidden tree. In other words, two trees can exist together uniformly on the exact same location so long as at least one of the trees is a "vine-tree," and vines were commonly trained onto fruit-trees when the Book of Genesis was composed. Such a practice was not confined to the Hebrews, as even the heathen nations exacted the same practice of training vines onto trees in order that two different kinds of fruit could be obtained from one source. Even the Romans, during the earthly days of Christ, considered vines to be trees. Such was once the situation with trained "trees" common to innumerable gardeners.

It is also important to note that wild vines exist parasitically by the strength of trees. Wild vines do not produce desirable fruit. Wild vines scale trees to obtain height in an effort to acquire the light and water necessary to sustain themselves. Wild vines often kill trees, for the bond between wild vines and trees produces enmity and competition for life. In fact, if one lets a wild vine scale one's own house, the wild vine can grow to such a stature that it constricts and ultimately crushes the house in a manner similar to a python's constriction. It is easy to comprehend why the ancients often compared vines to snakes.

We may note that English *Bibles* translate the word ערל to mean "forbidden" (which it indicates in Leviticus 19:23) when this word means, literally, "uncircumcised," i.e. unpruned. It is not difficult to understand why the ancients sometimes compared a vine and its clusters to anatomical masculinity; therefore, the act of a man's physical circumcision was held in a similar regard to the act of pruning a vine. Vines are pruned in order to promote fruit production; consider the fact that male babies were to be circumcised on the eighth day (Leviticus 12:3), and the letters שמנה can be pronounced to mean *fertile* or *eight*. Deuteronomy 10:16; 30:6, Jeremiah 4:4 and Romans 2:29 state that circumcision is truly of the "heart," for Genesis 17:11 explicitly states that the actual removal of the foreskin is only the "sign" of the covenant, the sign of an internal reduction and subsequent humility that leads to growth and fruitfulness. Since the word for לבב *heart* is the same word as "*mind*," we understand that a circumcised heart is the same as a pruned (and therefore a positively fruitful, humble) *mind*, which explains more of the nature of the Tree of the *Knowledge* of Good and Evil and the pride required to eat of it... for Satan is "king over all the children of pride," (Job 41:34) whereas "God resists the proud, but gives grace to the humble," (Proverbs 3:34: James 4:6; I Peter 5:5). Accordingly, it follows that a forbidden tree (vine) is an uncircumcised tree (vine); an uncircumcised tree (vine) is an unpruned tree (vine); an unpruned vine can become a fruitless vine quickly, and a fruitless tree is a barren tree. With respect to progeny, a fruitless human is a childless human, and when Abram indicated that he himself was "childless" (Genesis 15:2), he said, literally, that he was ערירי *naked*, i.e. *bare*, hence the idea of barren trees in relation to childless humanity; Abram was ashamed of his *fruitlessness*, his *childlessness*, his *nakedness*. Again, Christ said,

> "Every plant which My heavenly Father has not planted will be UPROOTED," (Matthew 15:13).

The idea of "uprooting" in Matthew 15:13 above must be referring to the Hebrew root עקר *to uproot*; the word עקר *barren* or *sterile* comes from this root עקר *to uproot*. We have already understood that Abram was ashamed of his *nakedness*, that is, his *childlessness* due to the fact that his wife was עקר *barren* (Genesis 11:30). The Hebrew idea of "uprooting" is intimately connected to "barrenness" and "sterility," just as the concepts of "nakedness" and "childlessness" are connected. Consider Joseph's words in Genesis 42:9 when he discussed the ערות הארץ *nakedness of the land*, that is, *the shameful barrenness of the land* that suffered *famine*. A "naked" land was a land that did not bear fruit. The first command God gave to humanity was to "Be fruitful and multiply..." (Genesis 1:28). Unfruitful people (like a land that suffered famine) were "naked" people (like the "nakedness" of the land that Joseph discussed). A fruitless womb and fruitless land were once thought of similarly, just as the world over considered fruitful land to be fertile.

The painful difficulty to bear human fruit is a result of the punishment God placed upon humanity (Genesis 3:16). We cannot blame God for planting something that He did not plant any more than we can blame God for creating bombs by the fact that He created metal. We cannot blame God for creating seedless fruit-trees on Day Third of Creation when He did not. Having understood that an uncircumcised vine is, by definition, a "forbidden tree," it is helpful to recall that the Tree of the Knowledge of Good and Evil must have held seedless fruit. Knowing that an uncircumcised vine is the same as a forbidden tree, we can better understand why Deuteronomy 32:32-33 compares a poisonous vine to a venomous serpent. Since people are often compared to trees in Scripture, we can understand why Christ compared Himself, positively in righteousness, to both a snake (John 3:14) and The True Vine (John 15:1); let us consider the negative and parasitic opposite situation regarding the Enemy. The fact that Christ called Himself the "True Vine" admits that there is a false vine; the True Vine hung on a tree of death, and we should consider (antithetically) the false vine that hung on the Tree of Life in Eden.

> "For their vine is of the vine of Sodom and of the fields of Gomorrah; their grapes are grapes of gall; their clusters are bitter. Their wine is the poison of serpents, and the cruel venom of cobras," (Deuteronomy 32:32-33).

Considering the forbidden tree, that is, the poisonous vine, Job 20 tells us plainly that "Adam" vomited the venom of serpents that he swallowed after having partaken from the forbidden tree. Therefore, the facts that the forbidden tree brought death and caused Adam to vomit admit that the forbidden tree (the uncircumcised vine, like a venomous serpent) was not "good for food." In Genesis 3:6, it has been assumed that "the tree" under discussion, but which is not named, is the forbidden tree:

> "So when the woman saw that THE TREE was good for food, that it was pleasant to the eyes, and a tree desirable to make one wise, she took of its fruit and ate. She also gave to her husband with her, and he ate";

but this passage states that the tree under discussion was "good for food" when we know that the forbidden tree was not good for food, for if it was "good for food," then it would not have brought death, nor would its poison have caused Adam to vomit. Genesis 2:9 says that "every" tree that God made was "good for food," and knowing that the fruit from the trees that people were given by God to eat contained seed, the "good" food discussed in Genesis 2:9 must have been seed-bearing. Accordingly, knowing that God was not originally responsible for seedless, bad fruit, it is a contradiction to state that the forbidden tree alone is described in Genesis 3:6. "Seed," "fruit," and "progeny" are understood as related terms. The Text says that the vegetation that can be attributed to God was "good," (Genesis 1:12). The vegetable productions that can be attributed to God on Day Third of Creation had seed in them. God is the "Living God" as is illustrated by His productions that were designed for multiplicative perpetuity. The command given to humanity regarding what humanity was allowed to eat is precise and deliberate; let us note the superlatives:

> "And God said, 'See, I have given you EVERY herb that yields seed which is on the face of all the earth, and EVERY tree whose fruit yields seed; to you it shall be for food. Also, to EVERY beast of the earth, to every bird of the air, and to EVERYTHING that creeps on the earth, in which there is life, I have given EVERY green herb for

food'; and it was so," (Genesis 1:29-30).

We may notice that humanity was given food in distinction when compared to the food that was given to animals. Humanity was given food that had "seed" in it, whereas the beasts, the birds, and all creeping things, in which there was life were given greenery, but no "seed" is mentioned with respect to them. The employment of superlatives eliminates many variables quickly.

Humanity was given "EVERY herb that yields seed which is on the face of all the earth, and EVERY tree whose fruit yields seed" for food; however, we have already seen that every vegetable production that was yielded on Day Third of Creation had seed, and as such, can be attributed to God. Let us turn to the words of Christ again:

> "Every plant which My heavenly Father has not planted will be UPROOTED," (Matthew 15:13).

Again, the idea of "uprooting" in Matthew 15:13 must be referring to the Hebrew root עקר *to uproot.* The word עקר *barren* or *sterile* comes from this root עקר *to uproot.* So, when considering that every plant that the heavenly Father did not plant will be *uprooted,* we can understand that every plant which the heavenly Father did not plant will be *barren* or *sterile* (עקר). We also know that there is only One God, and only He can create. Furthermore, we know that nothing can be added to or subtracted from His creation (Ecclesiastes 3:14), so that any variances within His creation are only the results made possible through that which was already created. Therefore, that humanity was given "every herb that yields seed which is on the face of all the earth" means that no herb that can be linked to God was restricted from humanity, for "every herb" that God created had seed (Genesis 1:11-12). Again, that humanity was given "every tree whose fruit yields seed," means that no tree that can be linked to God was restricted from humanity, for "every tree" that God created had seed in its fruit (Genesis 1:11-12). Furthermore, all of the vegetation that God created was "good" (Genesis 1:11-12), and we cannot rightfully call the forbidden tree "good" when its very name combined "good" with "evil"; such a combination is an unclean mixture, an unholy mingling which opposes God's design for everything that God created "according to its kind."

Noting the superlatives, let us eliminate possibilities with respect to this passage:

> "And the Lord God commanded the man, saying, 'Of EVERY tree of the garden you may freely eat; but of the Tree of the Knowledge of Good and Evil you shall not eat, for in the day that you eat of it you shall surely die,'" (Genesis 2:16-17).

From Genesis 1:29-30, we recall that humanity was given "every tree whose fruit yields seed"; therefore, the fact that a tree was restricted means that its fruit did not yield seed, i.e. its fruit was barren and sterile. At the same time, we remember from Genesis 1:11-12 that all vegetation attributed to God's creation contained seed. Furthermore, we have already understood, whether from nature or from Scripture (Romans 1: 18-20) that the purpose of "seed" is life. Therefore, the fact that a "tree" was forbidden by God, when every tree that God created was "good" (Genesis 1:12), means that the forbidden tree was bad. The fact that a "tree" was forbidden by God, when "every" tree that God created had fruit that yielded seed (and therefore fruit that yielded life) means that the forbidden tree was seedless, and it, specifically, led to death, which is stated plainly in Genesis 2:16-17. The fact that the two central trees in Eden were opposites indicates that the opposite of the Tree of Life was not "knowledge," but rather death. When the Word of God stated that, "Every plant which My Heavenly Father has not planted will be uprooted," (Matthew 15:13), and when we ask ourselves, "Which plants were *not* planted by God?" — the answer is: those that had no seed; those that were not good; those that led to death.

A barren tree is a naked tree, and a naked human is childless human in the same way that Abram was עֲרִירִי *naked, childless* in Genesis 15:2; let us consider the synonymous shame that Adam and his wife experienced when they "knew" that they were עֵירֻמִּם *naked*... By the fact that every tree that can be attributed to God on Day Third of Creation had seed in its fruit, every one of those trees had natural ability for sustentation and perpetuity. Thus, the first command God gave to humanity was to "Be fruitful and multiply..." (Genesis 1:28). Regarding fruit, fruitful multiplication is impossible with seedless fruit; seedless fruit is the result of mixing unlike entities. Good and Evil are unlike; therefore, the Tree of the Knowledge of Good and Evil was a tree of two unlike things that was, by definition, seedless and עָרֵל *forbidden, uncircumcised*. Knowing that the forbidden tree was seedless and discordant (for good and evil cannot be mixed according to their kind, but rather, despite their kind), and knowing that "everything" God made was "exceedingly good" (Genesis 1:31) indicates that God did not plant the forbidden tree.

CHAPTER FOUR

"ACCORDING TO ITS KIND"

We may observe the emphasis placed on the fact that God's creation was created "according to its kind," and it seeded seed "according to its kind":

On "Day Third":   "...God said, 'Let the earth bring forth grass, the herb that yields seed, and the fruit tree that yields fruit ACCORDING TO ITS KIND, whose seed is in itself, on the earth'; and it was so. And the earth brought forth grass, the herb that yields seed ACCORDING TO ITS KIND, and the tree that yields fruit, whose seed is in itself ACCORDING TO ITS KIND. And God saw that it was good..." (Genesis 1:11-12).

On "Day the Sixth":   "...God said, 'Let the earth bring forth the living creature ACCORDING TO ITS KIND: cattle and creeping thing and beast of the earth, each ACCORDING TO ITS KIND'; and it was so. And God made the beast of the earth ACCORDING TO ITS KIND, cattle ACCORDING TO ITS KIND, and everything that creeps on the earth ACCORDING TO ITS KIND. And God saw that it was good. Then God said, 'Let Us

> make man in Our image, according to
> Our likeness; let them have dominion
> over the fish of the sea, over the birds of
> the air, and over the cattle, over all the
> earth and over every creeping thing that
> creeps on the earth.' So God created
> man in His own image; in the image of
> God He created him; male and female
> He created them..." (Genesis 1:24-27).

Since such an emphasis is cast upon the individual likeness "according to its kind" of God's creation and its seed, it is evident that God was responsible for creating individually accordant uniqueness. However, good and evil do not, in any way, accord with each other; as such, the Tree of the Knowledge of Good and Evil could not have been "according to the kind" of something that preceded it. That is, such an inherent contradiction as the mingling of good and evil could not have been a component of the original creation. Let us turn again to Leviticus 19:19:

> "You shall keep My statutes. You shall not let your
> livestock breed with ANOTHER KIND. You shall not
> sow your field with MIXED SEED. Nor shall a garment of
> MIXED linen and wool come upon you."

Under the Torah, the idea of mixing breeds of animals, mingling a diversity of seed, or interweaving differing types of thread all conveyed a concept that called to remembrance the order of Creation. That is, every law that was ever established was established in reaction to something; therefore, to look only at a law's outward appearance, and to avoid considering the reasoning behind a law's outward appearance, is to perceive subjectivity arbitrarily, for religious prohibition against uncircumcised vines can be found even in the laws of Numa

Pompilius (8th – 7th Century B.C.) as recorded by Plutarch (*Britannica's Great Books*, Vol. 14, page 57).

It is apparent that the negative law(s) laid down in Leviticus 19:19 above originated with some breach of the natural order established in Creation. We have already observed a breach of the natural order when we consider the forbidden tree that was the product of two unlike entities [note 2, p. 170].

Having established that the forbidden tree was a mingling of unlike entities, and having determined that it could not have been seed-bearing, let us consider again "every" tree that can be attributed to God. On Day Third of Creation, God spoke, and the earth brought forth. Yet, the fact that the earth brought forth necessitates that God did something in accordance with His Word, and Genesis 2:9 proves this when it states,

> "And out of the ground the Lord God MADE EVERY TREE GROW that is pleasant to the sight and good for food..."

God made every tree grow that was pleasant to the sight and good for food. That the earth brought forth vegetation according to God's desire and that God made vegetation grow joins the reality that it is the bride who is to bring forth fruit to the reality that God created vegetation. In other words, the Creation "Days" in Genesis 1 emphasize femininity bringing forth fruit, and, as such, Day Third remains distinguished along such lines; at the same time, Genesis 2:9 explains the reality of vegetation that was brought forth by informing us with a little more as to how the growth happened. Therefore, Genesis 1 tells us that femininity brought forth, whereas Genesis 2:9 tells us that God "made" it so (specifically, for purposes under discussion, regarding "trees"). However, it has been a consistent tradition to blame the Word of God for supposed "contradictions" by stating that there are two different Creation accounts between Genesis 1 and Genesis 2, as if what we now call the first two chapters of the *Bible* are not according to the same kind but are differing accounts with equal historical validity! What? — how dare one blame the Hebrew Scriptures on account of the foreign, English wrinkles that were accidentally ironed into a translated dress! Nothing good can come from casting such a shadow on the veracity and consistency of God's Word; let us examine this point.

Genesis 1 states that the order of creation was (1) the division of light from the darkness, (2) the division of the waters, (3) the division of the water from the dry land and the sprouting of vegetation, (4) the celestial lights, (5) water creatures and winged creatures, and (6) land animals and man. It has been a common accusation that the order of the creation differs in Genesis 2 — and this assertion is beyond false and unfair. The problem has arisen because of the difficult qualifier in English versions of Genesis 2:5: "...and *no* tree of the field had yet appeared on the earth, and *no* plant of the field had yet sprung up..."; the problem with this **translation** is the superlative "no" when it is said that "no" tree of the field had yet appeared. The Torah says, literally, "וכל *and every* tree of the field was טרם *not yet* to be in the earth, וכל־עשב *and every herb* of the field had טרם *not yet* sprouted..." *The Stone Edition of the Tanach* renders this passage well when it states, "...now all the trees of the field were not yet on the earth and all the herb of the field had not yet sprouted..." The word "כל" can mean "all," "any" and "every," depending on the context in which it is employed, and being such a superlative, some English versions often select "any" (or "no," that is "none") instead of "every" and thus, accidentally, create an **English** contradiction that does not exist in the Hebrew Text. Therefore, the Creation on Day Third exhibited some (but not "every") form of vegetation, and the animal creation on Day Fifth and

Day the Sixth exhibited some (but not "every") form of animal life; these facts help to illustrate why both the inanimate life and the animate life were endowed with the capability to yield seed after their kind. Again, despite English translations, the Hebrew Scriptures do not say that "...He had rested from all His work which God created *and made*," (Genesis 2:3) but rather "which God created *to make*," that is, *to continue the production process*. The rudiments of Creation were completed first, and these rudiments were then followed by further specificity that allowed them to continue production. We have a repeat of the same situation with Noah:

> "And of every living thing FROM EVERY FLESH you shall bring two of every sort into the ark, to keep them alive with you; they shall be male and female. Of the birds AFTER THEIR KIND, of animals AFTER THEIR KIND, and of every creeping thing of the earth AFTER ITS KIND, two of every kind will come to you to keep them alive," (Genesis 6:19-20).

Surely the command quoted above must be referring to the prototypical creation, and not to the eventually mingled and cross-bread variants. First of all, a ship that was 450 feet long, 75 feet wide, and 45 feet high could not carry every known species in the entire world. Secondly, every known species in the entire world was not living exactly where Noah was living, as is true of any human being anywhere on the earth at any time. Thirdly, when we take into account that "every living thing FROM EVERY FLESH" was brought into the ark, we may notice that I Corinthians 15:39 states the exact same pattern as the directive given to Noah:

> "ALL FLESH IS NOT THE SAME FLESH, but there is one kind of flesh of men, another flesh of animals, another of fish, and another of birds,"

and here, listed before us, are the four major divisions of "flesh." These four divisions were divided again into "clean" and "unclean" animals; the clean animals were taken into the ark in sevens and the unclean animals were taken in pairs (Genesis 7:2). The animals were further divided into differing types of birds (Genesis 7:3), which is particularly pointed out in Genesis 8:7-8 when Noah utilized a raven and a dove.

> "On the very same day Noah and Noah's sons, Shem, Ham, and Japheth, and Noah's wife and the three wives of his sons with them, entered the ark — they and every beast AFTER ITS KIND, all cattle AFTER THEIR KIND, every creeping thing that creeps on the earth AFTER ITS KIND, and every bird AFTER ITS KIND, every bird of every sort. And they went into the ark to Noah, two by two, of all flesh in which is the breath of life. So those that entered, male and female of all flesh, went in as God had commanded him; and the Lord shut him in," (Genesis 7:13-16).

Nothing dead went into the ark, but all the "flesh" that went into the ark had the "breath of life." We may notice that neither humanity nor animal life was given meat to eat in Eden (1:29-30), that people prior to the flood of Noah's time were not given meat to eat (Genesis 1:29-30), that the "clean" animals were the animals fit for sacrifice (Genesis 8:20); then, humanity could eat of every kind of animal and sea creature (Genesis 9:2-3), the animals that were distinguished as "clean" for sacrifice were the animals that the Israelites specifically were allowed to eat as mandated by the Torah, and (on account of Salvation) a return to the manner of Abraham occurred regarding edible animals (Acts 10:15) that will be further reversed to the order of pre-fallen Eden in the Restoration (Isaiah 11). It is evident that the various "kinds" of flesh were not made up of every single species, but every single species was made up of the various kinds of flesh, as is indicated in

I Corinthians 15:39. It is written:

> "Now the sons of Noah who went out of the ark were Shem, Ham, and Japheth. And Ham was the father of Canaan. THESE THREE were the sons of Noah, and from these THE WHOLE EARTH WAS POPULATED," (Genesis 9:18-19).

Many from three is different than three from many. If every kind of human being descended from only three families who, in turn, descended from only one family, why would this same pattern not be true of the various "kinds" of animals? Regarding the creation in Genesis 1, some of the vegetation and some of the animals were created before man, but after man was created, then,

> "Out of the ground the Lord God formed EVERY beast of the field and EVERY bird of the air, and brought them to Adam to see what he would call them. And whatever Adam called each living creature, that was its name," (Genesis 2:19).

The rudiments of Creation were established before man, and these rudiments were endowed with the capability of reproduction. When God finished His Creation, he saw that "everything" He made was "very good," (Genesis 1:31). Genesis 2:3 states,

> "Then God blessed the seventh day and sanctified it, because in it He rested from all His work which God had created לעשות to make [i.e. created, so that it itself could produce]."

The total Creation was concluded after the creation of man, and it was created with the capability of perpetuity by seed. A key to this understanding is found in the fact that God commanded man to

"...HAVE DOMINION over the fish of the sea, over the birds of the air, and over every living thing that moves on the earth," (Genesis 1:28).

The fact that "dominion" is even discussed relative to animals and gardens indicates, with resounding specificity, that it is a פרדס *paradise* that is being discussed in the Eden narrative. Of course, Adam's garden home and Eden were two different places. Genesis 2:8 states that,

> "The Lord God planted a garden eastward IN Eden, and there He put the man whom He had formed."

That is, Adam's garden home was "ב *in*" Eden. Eden housed the garden, and the garden housed Adam. Accordingly, Genesis 2:10 states,

> "Now a river went out of Eden to water the garden, and from there it parted and became four riverheads."

That a river "went out of Eden" for the purposes of watering "the garden" illustrates that Eden in general cannot be the exact same place as the specific garden that it watered. The distinction between Eden and the garden home of Adam can be found in the definition of the word "garden" used in the Eden narrative. In Hebrew, the word גן *garden* comes from the root גנן *to defend, to guard*. Walls, thorns, moats, etc. were used to defend gardens and paradises when the Book of Genesis was composed, and the fact that the word גן *garden* is used in the Eden story indicates why

> "God took the man and placed him IN the Garden of Eden, to cultivate her and to שמר *guard* her," (Genesis 2:15).

The "Garden of Eden" (Genesis 3:23) was "in" Eden (Genesis 2:8), and Adam was to "guard" the garden (his home that was surrounded by a hedge).

A "paradise" was a kind of eastern Garden, and a "paradise" was, typically, the property of a King, hence the "dominion" under discussion. In other words, the term "paradise" has been misused by English speakers, and through its misuse, it has been restricted to indicate only an ethereal perfection when, in fact, a "paradise" was a specific type of eastern garden. A paradise was also enclosed within a wall. A difference between a "garden" and a "paradise" is that, even though they were both encompassed by a defense (wall, thorns, moats, etc.), a garden only housed inanimate life (plus the caretaker), whereas a paradise was stocked with animals. A paradise was a type of garden, but the prevailing distinction between a "garden" and a "paradise" was that only inanimate life (excepting the caretaker or caretakers) was found within a garden, but animate life was found within a paradise (aside from the caretaker or caretakers). We have such a distinction made by King Solomon when he stated that,

> "I made myself גנות gardens and פרדסים paradises, and I planted all kinds of fruit trees in them," (Ecclesiastes 2:5).

Paradises were, typically, owned by those who had "dominion," that is, by kings; it is partially for this reason that humanity was told to

> "...HAVE DOMINION over the fish of the sea, over the birds of the air, and over every living thing that moves on the earth," (Genesis 1:28).

Adam first lived within a garden that was within a paradise, and both his garden home and the paradise around it, by definition, had dividers or walls. Paradises can be thought of as a blend of gardens, orchards, and zoos that were fortified with protective walls or hedges; consider a vivarium. Since kings typically owned a country's paradises (and its waters), since paradises housed animal (and therefore animate) life, and since gardens were planted inside of paradises, it stands to reason, according to strict diction, theme, the order of creation, history, and God's specific command to "have dominion," that "Eden" was the "paradise" that housed Adam's "garden" home. That not "every" plant and not "every" animal were present before the creation of Adam, combined with the fact that, by definition, a garden had to have some sort of hedge or wall around it, and since animals were to be kept out of gardens, Adam could not have known (for a time) that the earth held other fleshly, animate life beyond himself; and this explains why Adam was "alone" (Genesis 2:18) and why it was then that God made "every" animal (Genesis 2:19). Since inanimate and animate life were created "according to its kind," and since it seeded seed "according to its kind," we can then understand how life began to spread out upon the earth [note 3, p. 170].

Since a garden housed inanimate life, and since a paradise housed animate life, we can understand why Song of Songs 4:12-13 refers to a woman as a "garden" in reference to a "paradise." How does one make a garden into a paradise? — by stocking the garden with animate life. How does a husband make his garden into a paradise? — by impregnating his wife. Let us not forget that "Eden" comes from the same root as עדנה *a womb that can produce fruit.*

> "A garden enclosed is my sister, my spouse, a spring shut up, a fountain sealed. Your plants are a פרדס *paradise* of pomegranates with pleasant fruits, fragrant henna with spikenard," (Song of Songs 4:12-13).

Again, consider the Living God as opposed to "the one who has the power of death, that is, the devil," (Hebrews 2:14). God created life, but the Enemy brought death. God planted a garden "in" Eden, and "Eden" can be understood in the same sense as a womb, for it is the womb where life is formed and, again, עדן *Eden* comes from the same root as עדנה *a womb that can produce fruit*. A garden can be turned into a paradise when animate life is put into a garden, as is true for femininity. After humanity sinned, then Adam named his wife "**Life**." When the *Bible* was written, people were buried in gardens, but paradises housed animate life. Innocent blood that is shed (in specific) and a corpse (in general) buried in soil and not upon rock or some above-ground place constitute the Scriptural causation of accursed and defiled ground. We know that corpses were entombed in gardens and not in paradises; we know that the Eden Narrative is blatantly discussing a paradise, yet it only employs the word "garden"; we know that a pregnant woman was a paradise; therefore, when God announced the curse against the ground in Genesis 3:17, and we know that innocent blood that is shed (in specific) and a corpse (in general) buried in soil constitute the causation of defiled land, we might at first ask ourselves, "Where then was the corpse in Eden?" and "Whose corpse was it?" Gardens housed inanimate life (vegetation and, sometimes, human corpses) plus the caretaker(s). When Mary Magdalene came to Christ's rock tomb (that was in a garden), the remaining component of the garden that she would have anticipated (beyond vegetation and Christ's corpse) was the gardener himself. Therefore, we can discern why Mary Magdalene came to the tomb and mistook the resurrected Christ as only a gardener (John 20:15-16). Anatomically speaking, in the same way that the situation of an innocent human slaughtered within a garden contradicts the consistent definition of a "paradise," so also to claim that the Living God planted a means of death in "Eden" contradicts the consistent definition of the "Eden" that God Himself planted. God could not have planted the forbidden tree.

CHAPTER 5

"THE TREE" OF GENESIS 3:6

We may notice that the "Tree of Life" was not discussed until the completion of the six Creation "Days" and the seventh "Day" that was the Sabbath. Names are important. Let us consider the fact that יוֹם *Day* is a proper noun, a title, a name in Genesis 1:3-5:

> "Then God said, 'Let there be light'; and there was light. And God saw the light, that it was good; and God divided the light from the darkness. God CALLED THE LIGHT 'DAY,' and the darkness He called 'Night.' So the evening and the morning were the first day."

The "light" was good, and it was divided from the darkness. Good and evil are antithetical to each other, for they are of different kinds; the mixture of these two is entirely ruinous (Ecclesiastes 10:1). Since a good-and-evil mixture produces nothing good, and since the "light" was "good," it stands to reason why it was divided from the darkness. Seedless fruit is produced by mixing two unlike entities. Seedless fruit cannot be fruitful; its fruit is unto itself; we may note again the "unfruitful works of darkness" (Ephesians 5:11) in contrast to "...bearing fruit in every good work, growing in the knowledge of God," (Colossians 1:10). When we reflect on the fact that Genesis 4:1 uses the word "he knew" to indicate the copulative union discussed in Genesis 2:24, we can then comprehend that the Tree of the Knowledge of Good and Evil was a tree of the union of good and evil, a tree of the union of unlike entities that was therefore seedless and bestowed an equivalent status upon those who partook of it despite their union, their knowledge... which is why such an unfruitful status was conquered by the prophecy of "Seed" in Genesis 3:15. The tree of the union of unlike entities brought about darkness in the midst of the light of life; Song of Songs 7:3 refers to a woman's navel as a אגן *goblet*, a *cup*, and offspring is compared to האגנות *the bowls* in Isaiah 22:24, for the words *cup* and *bowl* are the same; consider the golden bowl that served as an oil reservoir that fueled the branches of a burning lamp (Ecclesiastes 12:6), a flaming tree.

The name of light was "Day." The name of darkness was "Night." "Day" was "good." Again, "Day" was the name of the light; therefore, "Day" One is the same as saying "Light" one. The fact that there are seven "Days" discussed regarding Creation and the Sabbath mandates that there are seven "lights" discussed. The lamp-stand of seven lights is called the "menorah," which is understood as a tree on account of its "flowerlike cups," its "buds," its "blossoms," and its "branches," (Exodus 25:31-32), and we may therefore note that after the seven "Days" (lights) are discussed, it is only then that a "Tree of Life" is discussed, for the menorah is a tree of light (a tree of life). Man is sometimes compared to an olive tree (compare Romans 11 to the imagery of Zechariah 4); hence, Christ's statement: "You are the light of the world..." (Matthew 5:14), for the oil used for their lamps came from olives. When considering man, olive trees, and the menorah, we may observe their connection in Revelation 11:3-4:

> "'Also, I will give power to MY TWO WITNESSES; and they will prophesy for 1,260 days, dressed in sackcloth.' THESE ARE THE TWO OLIVE TREES and THE TWO MENORAHS standing before the Lord of the earth."

We have understood that "seed" and "fruit" can refer to progeny. We have comprehended that the Scriptures compare humans to olive trees, which is where the oil for lamps was derived. We may, therefore, understand that a tree of light is a tree of life, for the Scriptures continually interchange "light" and "life" or use "light" to parallel "life" (Psalm 36:9; 49:18-19; 56:13, etc.)* [note 4, p. 170]. Therefore, a tree of light is a tree of life, which helps to explain why, when regarding the figuration of words in Scripture, it is apparent that the word "lamp" is used to indicate "understanding" and an "heir" in I Kings 11:36, etc., why the expression, "To give him always a light [lamp]" in II Kings 8:19 means "to give him an heir to sit on his throne," and why the expression, "You will light my lamp" (Psalm 18:28) means "He will give me light and happiness; He will give me an heir"; the entire passage reads,

> "For You will light my lamp; the Lord my God will enlighten my darkness."

When we think of God's first words in Genesis ("Let there be light"), the "light" under discussion probably indicates "life," for the entire world was then ordered and stocked with life following this command for "light."

Since we have already seen that "light" and "life" are held in parallel, we may note that Ecclesiastes 7:11-12 states that "wisdom" gives "life." Light and life are characteristics of wisdom. Furthermore, since we have understood the indications of "seed" and "fruit" in relation to "progeny," it is no wonder that the Hebrew letter "ב" (which is the Hebrew number "2") is understood as both a "house" and "wisdom." The name of the letter ב is בית *a house*. A woman (generally) and a womb (specifically) are referred to as a "house" in Scripture repeatedly, which is a reason why it is written that God "built" (ויבן) the woman in Genesis 2:22, like a man "builds" a house.

In fact, Exodus 25:26-27 states that the "four" rings on the table of the showbread were "houses" for the poles that were inserted through them, thus relating the male-female union or the copulative "knowledge." The ancient Jews used to teach their children the alphabet (alephbet) by referring to the letter ב as "wisdom" (*Talmud: Shabbat*).

Since the letter ב signifies a "house," a "womb," and "wisdom," we can see a remarkable connection among these three entities in that Genesis 2:22 states that God "built" (from the root בנה pronounced Ba-Nah) the woman; the Hebrew word for a "son" is בן (pronounced BaNe), and a word for "wisdom" is pronounced בינה Bee-Nah; for all three ideas come from the letters B ב *womb* and N נ *son*, as is true of the word בין (pronounced BaNe = *between*) *midst* or *middle* (consider בתוך) where the forbidden Tree of the *Knowledge* of Good and Evil was in *Eden* (i.e. the *Fertile Womb*); for "son" is from the root "to build (as a house)" and the words "wisdom" and "midst" discussed above are from the root "to understand." Therefore, a "womb" and "wisdom" were understood to be intimately connected. A similar concept appears in English, for English speakers describe someone "thinking" by saying that someone is "conceiving," for "thought" and "conception" are synonyms.

God "built" the woman in Genesis 2:22 as a wise master builder builds a house... as One builds a family (I Chronicles 17:10)... and we must also recall that when the "House of God" is mentioned in Scripture, the Text refers to His temple; followers of Christ are the bride of Christ (2 Corinthians 11:2), and it stands to reason why the bride of Christ is also His "body" (Ephesians 5:22-24) and his "temple" because "God's Spirit lives within" His followers (I Corinthians 3:16). Such imagery can be understood more clearly when we read of how the act of slaying one's own child ("seed") defiles God's "sanctuary" (Leviticus 20:3), and how a "father's nakedness" or "father's skirt" refers to that father's wife (Genesis 9:22; Leviticus 20:11; Deuteronomy 27:20; Ezekiel 22:10); that is, the *nakedness of a man* also indicated the *flesh of his wife*; conversely, the *nakedness of a wife* could then also refer to *a man's flesh* (consider Hebrews 10:20 where the veil to the Holy of Holies is called Christ's *flesh*, for the word פרכת *veil* comes from the root פרך *to break*, as is true of a man's nakedness, i.e. his bride's flesh, in the covenant of marriage). Therefore, a priest in his temple is understood as a man in his wife.

> "The man who lies with HIS FATHER'S WIFE has uncovered HIS FATHER'S NAKEDNESS; both of them shall surely be put to death. Their blood shall be upon them," (Leviticus 20:11).

The "sanctuary" is the "bride," just as God "built" the woman (like a house) in Genesis 2:22. The construction of the Tabernacle was supposed to recall the "building" of the woman in Eden. Consider that God's house, the tabernacle in the wilderness, had a bridal train that hung from the rear of it (Exodus 26:12) and was led throughout the wilderness, as in a royal marriage procession, by a "pillar of cloud by day" (Numbers 14:14).

> "Who is this coming out of the WILDERNESS like PILLARS OF SMOKE, perfumed with myrrh and frankincense, with all the merchant's fragrant powders? Behold, it is Solomon's couch, with sixty valiant men around it, of the valiant of Israel. They all hold swords, being expert in war. Every man has his sword on his thigh because of fear in the night. Of the wood of Lebanon Solomon the King made himself a *palanquin* [*like the Holy Ark with its poles*]: he made its pillars of silver, its support

of gold, its seat of purple, its interior paved with love by the daughters of Jerusalem. Go forth, O daughters of Zion, and see King Solomon with the crown with which his mother crowned him on the day of his WEDDING, the day of the gladness of his heart," (Song of Songs 3:6-11).

Consider Jeremiah 2:1-2:

"The Lord spoke His word to me, saying: Go and speak to the people of Jerusalem, saying: This is what the Lord says: 'I remember how faithful you were to me when you were a young nation. You loved me like a young bride. You followed me through the desert, a land that had never been planted.'"

Let us digress for a moment to consider the "palanquin" discussed above. In Ginsburg's commentary on the Song of Songs, he wrote, "Palanquins were and are still used in the East by great personages. They are like a couch, sufficiently long for the rider to recline, covered with a canopy resting on pillars at the four corners, hung round with curtains to exclude the sun; they have a door, sometimes a lattice-work on each side. They are borne by four or more men, by means of strong poles," (p. 152). The word אפריון *palanquin* (rendered "chariot," and "bed") above is derived from the root פרה *to be fruitful*, hence its bed-like construction. The holy ארון *ark* is from the root ארה *to gather*, and this root produces the words "stall," "stable," and "lion." As palanquins had a lattice-work on each side, we may reflect on the crown that surrounded the Ark (Exodus 25:11). Palanquins were supported by poles, as was true of the Ark (Exodus 25:14). Palanquins were covered by a canopy, and the top of the Ark was covered by the wings of the cherubs (Exodus 25:20). Palanquins were like chariots, and the Ark was known as a chariot (I Chronicles

28:18). In any case, the procession of the tabernacle through the wilderness, the pillar of cloud, and the Holy Ark were all arranged comparably to a royal marriage procession, like the one discussed in Song of Songs 3. It is useful to remember that God filled the craftsmen "with the Spirit of God, in חכמה *wisdom* [consider its synonym שכל], in understanding, in knowledge, and in all manner of workmanship, to design artistic works, to work in gold, in silver, in bronze, in cutting jewels for setting, in carving wood, and to work in all manner of workmanship" (Exodus 31:3-5) in order to "build" the Tabernacle, the Bride. We may understand such a marriage procession in the sense of walking in covenant. That is, as a bride walks with her husband, so mankind is to walk with God.

Having observed that the concepts of "wisdom," "building," a "house," "light," and a "womb" all encompass the idea of life in the letter ב, it is no wonder that first statement of the *Bible* (Genesis 1:1) utilizes this letter as the first letter of the first sentence to explain creation. Accordingly, the first letter of the New Testament's first Book is the Greek equivalent of the Hebrew "ב" (or "2") which is "B" (or "2" as well): "The *book* of the GENERATIONS of Jesus Christ..." (Matthew 1:1).

Again, the name of the letter ב is בית *a house*. A woman and a womb are referred to as a "house," and the ancient Jews used to teach the alphabet (alephbet) by referring to the letter ב (the *house*) as "wisdom." Consider that it was King Solomon, the wise, who built the house of God. That the letter ב indicated both a "house" and "wisdom" explains the imagery of the "wise master builder" found in 1 Corinthians 3:10. The idea that a tree of light is a tree of life, and knowledge that a "womb" is understood in the same sense as "wisdom" helps us to comprehend why Ecclesiastes 7:11-12 states that "wisdom" gives "life" relative to the comparison made between "inheritance," and the "sun," for these descriptions are built around the ב *womb*:

> "WISDOM is good with an INHERITANCE, and profitable to those who see the SUN. For wisdom is a defense as money is a defense, but the excellence of knowledge is that WISDOM GIVES LIFE to those who have it."

When we reflect on the "ground" that is to bring forth fruit (as is the case with the womb) in conjunction with the fact that a womb was also thought of as a "house," we can then reasonably deduce that "womb" = "house" = "ground" in terms of **life** by way of allusion.

> "You shall not covet your neighbor's WIFE; and you shall not desire your neighbor's HOUSE, his FIELD..." (Deuteronomy 5:21).

A woman's womb is Scripturally paralleled to the earth that is to bear fruit, and we can notice such a parallel (procreation and vegetable production) in Psalm 139:13-15:

> "For You formed my inward parts; You covered me IN MY MOTHER'S WOMB. I will praise You, for I am fearfully and wonderfully made; marvelous are Your works, and that my soul knows very well. My frame was not hidden from You, when I was made in secret, and skillfully wrought IN THE LOWEST PARTS OF THE EARTH."

We know that a "lamp" and a "light" can refer to an heir (and therefore an inheritance, that is, "seed," and "fruit"). We have understood that a "garden" can refer to a woman. We have understood that a "paradise" can refer to a pregnant woman. We have understood that birth indicates a lamp, a light, an heir, etc. Accordingly, the link to the illustrations in

I Corinthians 3:1-15 becomes apparent:

> "And I, brethren, could not speak to you as to spiritual people but as to carnal, as to BABES in Christ. I fed you with milk and not with solid food; for until now you were not able to receive it, and even now you are still not able; for you are still carnal. For where there are envy, strife, and divisions among you, are you not carnal and behaving like mere men? For when one says, 'I am of Paul,' and another, 'I am of Apollos,' are you not carnal? Who then is Paul, and who is Apollos, but ministers through whom you believed, as the Lord gave to each one? I PLANTED, Apollos WATERED, but God gave the increase. So then neither he who PLANTS is anything, nor he who WATERS, but God who gives the increase. Now he who PLANTS and he who WATERS are one, and each one will receive his own reward according to his own labor. For we are God's fellow workers; you are God's FIELD, you are God's BUILDING [consider: "You shall not covet your neighbor's WIFE; and you shall not desire your neighbor's HOUSE, his FIELD..." (Deuteronomy 5:21)]. According to the grace of God which was given to me, as a WISE MASTER BUILDER I have laid the foundation, and ANOTHER BUILDS on it. But let each one take heed how he BUILDS on it. For no other FOUNDATION can anyone lay than that which is laid, which is Jesus Christ. Now if anyone BUILDS ON THIS FOUNDATION with gold, silver, precious stones, wood, hay, straw, each one's work will become clear; for the Day will declare it, because it will be revealed by fire; and the fire will test each one's work, of what sort it is. If anyone's work which he has BUILT on it endures, he will receive a reward. If anyone's work is burned, he will suffer loss; but he himself will be saved, yet so as through fire. Do you not know that

you are the TEMPLE of God and that the Spirit of God dwells in you?"

We have recognized that it is the man who plants his seed, and it is the bride who brings forth fruit, which helps explain why it was the woman who gave Adam the forbidden fruit and not Adam who gave it to her (Genesis 3:6). We grasp that "light" can indicate enlightenment just as "wisdom" is linked to "light." Therefore, it was the Tree of Life (the tree of light) that gave wisdom; for, according to strict logic, the forbidden tree could not have given wisdom since wisdom gives **life** (Ecclesiastes 7:11-12) and the forbidden tree gave death.

The Scriptures tell us that the Tree of Life and the Tree of the Knowledge of Good and Evil were both in the "middle" of the garden, and we know that God did not plant the Tree of the Knowledge of Good and Evil. Seedless fruit is produced by mixing two opposites, two incongruent, that is, two unlike things; good and evil are complete opposites. Death is the opposite of Life. The forbidden tree was the opposite of the Tree of Life, and it is a contradiction to say that the forbidden tree held "wisdom"; that is, since the two central trees of Eden were opposites, it cannot be that "wisdom" was the opposite of "life" when Proverbs 3:18 says that "wisdom" is a "tree of life." Death is the opposite of life; therefore, a tree of death is the opposite of the Tree of Life. The Tree of the Knowledge of Good and Evil must have been a deadly vine which indicates more of why Deuteronomy 32:32-33 compares a poisonous vine to a venomous snake.

The tree of light, the menorah, is a tree that is on fire and is yet not consumed by the fire. Proverbs 3:8 says that "wisdom" is a "tree of life." Ecclesiastes 8:1 indicates that the result of "wisdom" is "light." Ecclesiastes 2:13 says that "wisdom excels folly as light excels darkness." Ecclesiastes 7:12 says that "wisdom" gives "life." Genesis 3:6 states,

> "So when the woman saw that THE TREE was good for food, that it was pleasant to the eyes, and a tree desirable to make one wise, she took of its fruit and ate. She also gave to her husband with her, and he ate."

If it is assumed that "the tree" under discussion in Genesis 3:6 is the forbidden tree, we may therefore note the following contradictions:

(1) Genesis 3:6 states that "the tree" the woman saw was "good for food"; however, having already established that the forbidden tree caused vomiting (Job 20) and death (Genesis 3:19), it could not have been "good for food." Having already established that it was seedless, it cannot be attributed to God. Having only two trees with proper names to choose from in this case, the fact that "the tree" was "good for food" necessitates that "the tree" being discussed was the Tree of Life.

(2) Genesis 3:6 states that "the tree" was "תאוה enticing לעינים to the eyes" (Genesis 3:6); however, "every tree" that God caused to grow was "נחמד pleasant למראה to the sight" (Genesis 2:9), not "תאוה enticing לעינים to the eyes." Having only two trees with proper names to choose from in this case, the fact that "the tree" was "enticing to the eyes" necessitates that "the tree" being discussed was the Tree of the Knowledge of Good and Evil.

Both Adam and his wife, who was named חוה Life after she was "deceived and fell into transgression" (I Timothy 2:14), were certainly not deceived. Adam "was not deceived," (I Timothy 2:14). Therefore, Adam willingly permitted his wife to err, and he himself willfully rebelled against God (as was true of King Solomon, the wise). The woman was deceived, and ambiguity leads to confusion. It was the woman who was deceived and who took up discourse with the "serpent"; and having been deceived, she erred. It is no wonder that, in describing the woman's confused discourse with the "serpent" (where she misquoted God in Genesis 3:2-3), the Text itself ceases from using the proper names of the two central trees. Ambiguity can cause confusion, just as assumption can do the same. The man was not deceived; the woman was deceived; the followers of Christ are referred to as His bride. It is good to remember that it is the man who is to yield seed, and it is the bride who is to bring forth fruit; this unified process is only possible if the two become one (Genesis 2:24). The word דעת knowledge, as in the Tree of the Knowledge of Good and Evil, comes from the root ידע he knew; it is written that Adam "was not deceived" (I Timothy 2:14).

English-speakers often call a leafless tree a "naked" tree. However, keeping with a Biblical Hebrew expression (since we are discussing the Hebrew Bible), barrenness was often expressed as nakedness; therefore, a "naked" human was fruitless in the same way that Abram was ערירי naked, childless in Genesis 15:2; let us consider the shame that Adam and his wife experienced when they "knew" that they were עירמם naked... The process of the production of human fruit (called "knowing" in Scripture: Genesis 4:1) is only possible if the male and female become one. It cannot be that intercourse was the first human sin when the first command given to humanity was to be "fruitful" and to "multiply" (Genesis 1:28). That "wisdom" and "knowledge" are even discussed in relation to the Enemy in a "garden" would, of necessity, indicate something to do with the spread of humanity through birth (the result of "knowing") and subsequent procreation — as is the entire theme of the Eden narrative relative to the word "garden," the names of the "rivers," the fact that there were "four" of them, because "fruit" and "nakedness" were central to the topic, and since "Eden" comes from the same root as "a viable womb." A prevailing concept is unity. Again, the word אחד can be pronounced to produce the words *one* (Genesis 1:5) and *to unite* (Ezekiel 21:21), so we can see why "light" was, ironically, *divided* from "darkness" on Day *One* [The Day of *Union*]... for "light" was "good" (Genesis 1:4) and death was not. Regarding the Tree of the *Knowledge* [*Union*] of Good and Evil, we may understand that the forbidden tree was a product of the *union*... the marriage... the binding together... the mixture, that is, the *knowledge* of unlike entities... God separated light from darkness, whereas Satan connected light with darkness, as did humanity... and here we begin to see the taint passed down from parent to child.

It cannot be that "the tree" discussed in Genesis 3:6 was exclusively the forbidden tree. Since we know that the forbidden "tree" was certainly not good for food, we must rule out the possibility of the forbidden tree's advantageousness when the Narrative says that the woman saw that the tree was good for food. That is, since we know that the woman was deceived (I Timothy 2:14), then what she "saw" (Genesis 3:6) would have been less than accurate; however, what we may see from the Narrative after the fact, despite the woman's *personal* misconception as the story took place, can help us to understand how and why she was deceived. Since we know that "wisdom" brings "life" (Ecclesiastes 7:12), and since the forbidden tree brought death, it cannot be that the forbidden tree was "desirable to make one wise," despite what the woman saw (or thought she saw).

"The tree" under discussion is only possible if two "trees" are being observed simultaneously.

Genesis 2:9 states that the Tree of Life was in the "middle" of the garden. However, Genesis 3:3 states that the forbidden tree was in the "middle" of the garden, and the Text systematically ceases using proper names regarding trees. The situation of two trees discussed as one is only possible with the situation of a "vine-tree" wrapped around (or binding) a "tree"; since such was a common gardening practice when Genesis was first penned, we can better understand the situation of the two central trees appearing as one, for the vine's shape, of necessity, must conform to the tree's shape on which it hangs in order for it to exist with the tree. Consider the burial wrappings and the corpse of Lazarus; such wrappings, by nature, must conform to the body, but they are not the body itself. Ultimately, we can see why Christ made it a specific point to discuss the *bindings* of death when, regarding Lazarus, Christ said, "*Loose* him, and let him go," (John 11:44), for such *bindings* were once understood as illustrations of death. We may grasp the death/binding (pythonic) figure when we observe that Hebrews 11:19 refers to such a binding as death itself. That is, Hebrews 11:19 states that God "...was able to raise him [Isaac] up, even from the dead; from whence also he received him in a figure [i.e. figuratively]," for it is written that Abraham "*bound* Isaac his son" (Genesis 22:9). The point is this: Genesis 22:9 states that Abraham "bound" his son, but the emphatic turn of events was that Isaac was not killed; yet, when Hebrews 11:19 recounts the story of Isaac's binding, Hebrews 11:19 speaks as if Isaac was indeed killed. We may therefore grasp that, in the case of Isaac, Lazarus, and the forbidden tree, "binding" was understood in the sense of death. The opposite of the Tree of Life was a tree of death. There is only one kind of tree that can "bind" another tree, and such a rope-like tree is what Scripture calls a "vine-tree." Accordingly, the midst of Eden (during Adam's decision to sin) was a display of life wrapped about by death in that the Tree of Life was bound by the tree of death like a man bound by a serpent.

> "Moreover I saw under the sun: In the place of judgment, wickedness was there; and in the place of righteousness, iniquity was there," (Ecclesiastes 3:16).

Again, it is written,

> "Wisdom is good with an inheritance, and profitable to those who see the sun. For wisdom is a defense as money is a defense, but the excellence of KNOWLEDGE is that WISDOM GIVES LIFE to those who have it," (Ecclesiastes 7:11-12).

To assume that a tree of death could give wisdom is to be guilty of a contradiction. God did not plant the forbidden tree, for the tree that was "desirable to make one wise" (Genesis 3:6) was the Tree of Life from which people were permitted to eat prior to the great Fall of humanity. The Tree that was enticing to the eyes was the forbidden tree of death, the Tree of the Knowledge of Good *and* Evil, and such a mixture of good and evil is entirely ruinous (Ecclesiastes 10:1). Adam was supposed to *know* his wife according to the very first commandment given to humanity in Genesis 1:28, and where a use is possible, an abuse is also possible, hence the figure of "whoring" away to sin used repeatedly in Scripture.

Even though Ecclesiastes 2:13 says that "wisdom excels folly as light excels darkness," we must remember that "...a little folly outweighs wisdom and honor," (Ecclesiastes 10:1). The name of light is "Day," and the name of darkness is "Night"; Amos 5:8 refers to "Night" as "the shadow of death" (as is true consistently in Job). "The tree" in the "middle" of Eden was a "tree" that was coiled about by a poisonous "vine-tree"; the woman saw two trees simultaneously in exactly the same way we observe vines on trees today. If every aspect of what the woman saw is applied to the forbidden tree by us, endless contradictions arise. It is advantageous to understand that the word "good" used in the "Tree of the Knowledge of Good and Evil" is also the word for "beauty" (Exodus 2:2) and the word "evil" employed here is also the word for "injury" and "harm" (Genesis 31:52), for the forbidden tree surely injured the original beauty established by God, according to God's design that was ordered to produce viable fruit. Again, when Genesis was first penned, it was a common practice to train vines onto trees. Furthermore, even in wild nature today, wild (unpruned/uncircumcised/forbidden) vines thrive by climbing trees. Ecclesiastes 2:13 parallels "wisdom" to "light" and "folly" to "darkness," and we may understand "wisdom" in parallel to "Day" and darkness in parallel to "Night"; knowing that "Night" is understood to indicate "the shadow of death," we can comprehend the antithesis (that "Day" is understood as "life"). Since "life" is synonymous to "light," then we understand a tree of light as opposed to a tree of darkness, or the Tree of Life as opposed to the tree of death, i.e. the Tree of Life as opposed to the Tree of the Knowledge of Good and Evil. "The tree" of Genesis 3:6 was a situation of two trees: a tree of longevity coiled about by a vine of venom... life wrapped about by death. Even up to the time of the agriculturalist Columella (1st Century A.D.), the situation of a vine trained onto a tree was proverbially understood as a wedding — the marriage of the vine and tree (Columella, On Agriculture; Book III: note). A negative application of such a principle, concerning a poisonous vine, is easily understood as a marriage where the fruit thereof is deathly.

CHAPTER SIX

EATING & DRINKING

That words have definite meanings is certain, and a dictionary is essential to the study of language. At the same time, the manner in which words are used is the other half of diction study, and one will notice the peculiarity with which Scripture employs its vocabulary. For example, the word signifying that somebody אכל *ate* something is used in many contexts. To "eat" can indicate the simple consumption of food (Genesis 2:16), the "burning" of something (Ezekiel 15:4), a sword's "slaying" capability (II Samuel 18:8), and the overall "destruction" of something or someone (Numbers 16:45); in fact, Numbers 14:9 uses the word לחם *bread* to refer to *people* who are to be destroyed (eaten). Thus, in each of the preceding descriptions of "eating," the idea conveyed is one of breakdown.

However, a distinct, yet common, idiomatic application of the term "eating" denoted the acquisition and digestion of knowledge. The One who created man is also the One who dictated Scripture. Regarding the creation of Adam, it is written literally that, "the Lord God יצר *formed (as a potter)* the man from the dust of the אדמה *ground...*" and ancient eastern potters were often book-makers. When we take into account that some of the oldest books in the world were made by impressing tiny words upon clay tablets that were subsequently baked like bread in order to harden the clay surface, it becomes easier to grasp how the imagery of bread in an oven became used to illustrate the process of making books by way of a potter, for in this sense, the Potter, our God, created, fed, and composed — and we may begin to grasp the symbolism in the creation Narrative in which pottery, food, and knowledge are key factors. The Hebrew לחם means *bread*, *food*, and *fruit* (Jeremiah 11:19). As bread was eaten, so words were to be understood. The writing on clay tablets hardened in ovens would have become obscured and even destroyed upon baking had the expansion of the clay not been prevented by the potter, and we may comprehend part of the significance of unleavened bread. Furthermore, such clay books were often written in such small letters that it required a magnifying lens both to produce and to read them; thus, one's *eyes needed to be opened* by a lens in order to obtain the knowledge within, and we may reflect on the words of the "serpent" in Genesis 3 along with the woman's oral inflation of God's Word. Some ancient, eastern "books" (or sets of public laws) were written on pillars, and so we may see in this the imagery of a "tree of knowledge" from which one could "eat," that is, from which one could learn. The same idea of "eating" knowledge carried over to the usage of scrolls. Accordingly, it is written:

> "... O Mortal, eat what is offered to you; EAT this SCROLL... Then I ate it; and in my mouth it was as sweet as honey," (Ezekiel 3:1-3);

> "Your WORDS were found, and I ATE them, and your words became to me a joy and the delight of my heart; for I am called by your Name, O Lord, God of Hosts," (Jeremiah 15:16).

> "Then I took the little BOOK out of the angel's hand and ATE it, and it was as sweet as honey in my mouth.

But when I had eaten it, my stomach became bitter,"
(Revelation 10:10).

The prevailing idea expressed in the three passages immediately above is that to "eat" words is to make the knowledge conveyed by them part of oneself. Woman was made from man. The man and the woman became one. Unfortunately, the original "good" and "beautiful" state of mankind became one with "evil" or "injury" through "eating" from the Tree of the "Knowledge" of Good and Evil. "Wisdom" is personified in the Proverbs and says, "Come, eat of my bread and drink of the wine I have mixed," (Proverbs 9:5), for consuming such a doctrine is beneficial since "...wisdom gives life to the one who possesses it," (Ecclesiastes 7:12). Christ said,

> "...I am the Bread of Life. Whoever comes to Me will never be hungry, and whoever believes in Me will never be thirsty," (John 6:35).

Dr. Bullinger pointed out the following concerning John 6:53:

> "'eat... drink', &c. The Hebrews used this expression with reference to knowledge by the... [*figure of*] Metonymy (of the Subject)... where it is put for being alive; so eating and drinking denoted the operation of the mind in receiving and 'inwardly digesting' truth or the words of God. See Deut. 8:3, and cp. Jer. 15:16. Ezek. 2:8. No idiom was more common in the days of our Lord. With them as with us, eating included the meaning of enjoyment, as in Ecc. 5:19; 6:2; for 'riches' cannot be eaten... The Lord's words could be understood thus by hearers, for they knew the idiom; but of 'the eucharist' they knew nothing, and could not have thus understood them. By comparing vv. 47 and

48 with vv. 53 and 54, we see that believing on Christ was exactly the same thing as eating and drinking Him," (*Companion Bible*, Bullinger; p. 1532).

Dr. Lightfoot pointed out the following concerning John 6:53:

"There was nothing more common in the schools of the Jews than the phrases of 'eating and drinking' in a metaphorical sense. And surely it would sound very harsh, if not to be understood here metaphorically, but literally... Bread is very frequently used in the Jewish writers for *doctrine*," (*Commentary on the New Testament from the Talmud and Hebraica,* Lightfoot, Vol. 3; p. 307-308).

We may therefore consider:

"Yet I planted you as a choice vine, from the purest stock. How then did you turn degenerate and become a wild vine?" (Jeremiah 2:21).

"You plant them, and they take root; they grow and bring forth fruit; you are near in their mouths yet far from their hearts," (Jeremiah 12:2).

According to Scriptural formula, "eating" something can mean physically consuming something, burning something, slaying something or someone, destroying something or someone, and understanding something by making it a part of one's own being. The first command given to humanity was to

"Be FRUITFUL and multiply; fill the earth and subdue it; have dominion over the fish of the sea, over the birds of the air, and over every living thing that moves on the earth," (Genesis 1:28).

If "fruit" is "eaten," then "fruit" can be bitten into and

subsequently swallowed, burned, slain, destroyed, or understood... depending on what manner of fruit is under discussion, and depending on the context. Again, it is written:

> "And the Lord God commanded the man, saying, 'Of EVERY tree of the garden you may freely eat; but of the Tree of the Knowledge of Good and Evil you shall not eat, for in the day that you eat of it you shall surely die,'" (Genesis 2:16-17).

The reader must ask, "If every tree of the garden was given to man that he may 'freely eat,' and if the forbidden tree was in the garden, then why could not man eat from the forbidden tree?" — which is the very implication of the Enemy's first words in the Eden narrative when, in Genesis 3:1, he asked,

> "Has God indeed said, 'You shall not eat of EVERY tree of the garden'?"

God did indeed say that "...of EVERY tree of the garden you may freely eat..." so the question appears to remain regarding why the humans could not eat of the forbidden tree since it was indeed in the garden, and in its very center. The word מָשַׁל means both *to rule* and *to riddle*; consider such a thematic relationship in Daniel 8:23: "And in the latter time of their kingdom, when the transgressors have reached their fullness, a *king* shall arise, having fierce features, who understands חִידוֹת *riddles*." The first words of the so-called "serpent" of Genesis 3 formed a riddle, for he sought to rule over humanity in opposition to God's intended design. God said to Cain, "If you do well, will you not be accepted? And if you do not do well, sin lies at the door. And its desire is for you, but you should *rule over* it," (Genesis 4:7).

If the man was permitted to eat "OF EVERY tree of the garden," but he was forbidden from a certain tree, then the forbidden tree could not have been "OF the garden"; but surely the forbidden tree was "IN the midst of the garden" (Genesis 2:9 substantiated by the fact that its "fruit" was there in Genesis 3:3-6). Therefore, we understand that the forbidden tree was "IN the midst of the garden" but that it was not "OF the garden"; that is, God commanded literally that humanity could eat "מכל עץ־הגן *from every tree* [OF] the garden," and He did not say "from every tree IN the garden." "God took the man and placed him IN the Garden of Eden, to עבדה *cultivate her* and to שמרה *guard her*," (Genesis 2:15). The man was placed "in" the garden, but even though the forbidden tree ended up "in" the garden, it was, distinctly, not "of" the garden; we may consider the exact opposite of this statement in I John 2:15-17, for before humanity ate of the forbidden tree, the forbidden tree was "in" but not "of" Adam's garden home... but after the great Fall, we are to be "in" but not "of" the world.

> "Do not love the world or the things IN the world. If anyone loves the world, the love of the Father is not in him. For all that is IN the world — the lust of the flesh, the lust of the eyes, and the pride of life — is not OF the Father but is OF the world. And the world is passing away, and the lust of it; but he who does the will of God abides forever."

The forbidden tree was decidedly "in" the middle of the garden, but was decidedly not "of" the garden in the same way that followers of Christ are "in" the world but not "of" the world. The (1) "lust of the flesh," the (2) "lust of the eyes," and the (3) "pride of life" discussed in I John 2:15-17 blatantly refer to Genesis 3:6 where it is stated that "...when the woman saw that the tree was [1] good for food, that it was [2] enticing to the eyes, and a tree desirable [3] to make one wise, she took of its fruit and ate. She also gave to her husband with her, and he ate." We may now consider the following:

"And out of the ground the Lord God made EVERY tree grow that is pleasant to the sight and good for food. The Tree of Life was [*also*] IN THE MIDST of the garden, and the Tree of the Knowledge of Good and Evil," (Genesis 2:9).

Literally, there is no word for "also" in the Hebrew passage above; it is written,

"And out of the ground the Lord God made EVERY tree grow that is pleasant to the sight and good for food; the Tree of Life was IN THE MIDST of the garden, and the Tree of the Knowledge of Good and Evil..."

and this passage was probably meant to end by the figure of Aposiopesis (sudden silence) that can be signified by an ellipsis (...) [note 5, p. 171] in today's English.

Let us deal with the first portion of Genesis 2:9. "Every" tree that the Lord God made to grow was both "pleasant to the sight and good for food." We can hardly provide any sound or consistent reason to assert that the forbidden tree was in any way "good for food" when we have already determined that it was seedless, not good, and that it lead to death; furthermore, Job 20 vividly describes Adam spewing this food out of his mouth through his own vomit. So, if "every" tree that the Lord God made to grow was *both* good for food "and" pleasant to the sight, then eliminating one of these two factors eliminates the possibility of God having created it. Furthermore, the forbidden tree was "תאוה *enticing* לעינים *to the eyes*" (Genesis 3:6), not "נחמד *pleasant* למראה *to the sight*" like "every" tree that God caused to grow (Genesis 2:9). All vegetation that can be attributed to God was seed-bearing, lawful for people to eat, good for food, and pleasant to the sight; the Tree of the Knowledge of Good and Evil was none of these things, which is why it cannot be attributed to God.

Let us deal with the second portion of Genesis 2:9. The fact that the forbidden tree was, eventually, "in the midst of the garden" (Genesis 2:9 in conjunction with Genesis 2:16-17 and Genesis 3:3) says nothing as to how it got there nor as to whom its planter was. It is written that "God took the man and placed him IN the Garden of Eden to עבדה *cultivate her* and to שמרה *guard her*," (Genesis 2:15); this means that there was something, or someone, for Adam to "guard" against. The reader must ask, "Who, or what, was Adam to guard against?" In so asking, we may, again, gain insight from Christ's statement, "Every plant which My Heavenly Father has not planted will be uprooted," (Matthew 15:13), connected to Matthew 13:24-30 concerning the plants that "an enemy" planted; and since the forbidden tree could not have been "of" the garden, but was "in" the very center of the garden, combined with the fact that Adam was to "guard" the garden, we can deduce that the forbidden tree was the result of an intrusion at most or a wicked allowance at least. Followers of Christ would do well to heed these words: "For what have I to do with judging those also who are outside? Do you not judge those who are inside? But those who are outside God judges. Therefore 'put away from yourselves the evil person,' [Deuteronomy 19:19; 21:21; 22:21, 24; 24:7]," (I Corinthians 5:12-13). Note the distinction between "outside" and "inside" relative to the fact that the word "garden" under discussion is from the root that indicates "defense" and therefore hedges, walls, etc. Observe how quickly wild (uncircumcised/forbidden) vines (trees) can scale a garden wall and penetrate property to the destruction of the property along with the fact that one of the most consistent intruders of ancient eastern gardens was the serpent.

Having determined that the forbidden tree was seedless, not good, and that it led to death, we can understand that it was the parasitic opposite of everything that God created that had "seed," was "good," and led to life. Knowing that seedless plants are the result of manipulations, and knowing that manipulations can only occur when there is something preexisting which can be manipulated, we may understand why the curse pronounced against the Enemy involved enmity between him and the woman, between his "seed" and her "Seed." Through the record of the judgment in Genesis 3, we gain better understanding of the emphatic usage of "seed." Consider again the first command given to humanity:

> "Then God blessed them, and God said to them, 'Be fruitful and multiply; fill the earth and subdue it; HAVE DOMINION OVER the fish of the sea, over the birds of the air, and over EVERY LIVING THING THAT MOVES ON THE EARTH,'" (Genesis 1:28).

The reader will notice that a reason for the judgment came about because humanity did not take "dominion over... EVERY living thing that moves on the earth," for, "...the Lord said to Satan, 'From where do you come?' So Satan answered the Lord and said, 'From going TO AND FRO ON THE EARTH, and from WALKING BACK AND FORTH ON IT,'" (Job 1:7). The very fact that the Enemy moved upon the earth meant that humanity was given authority to dominate the Enemy. Since humanity did not rule over Satan but instead decided to have Satan riddle and rule over them, we can, again, gain a better understanding of God's warning to Cain in Genesis 4:7:

> "If you do well, will you not be accepted? And if you do not do well, sin lies at the door. And its desire is for you, but you should RULE OVER IT."

The fact that the forbidden tree did not have seed, was not good for food, and led to death, combined with the reality that it was in the garden but not "of" the garden, on top of the fact that "every" tree that can be attributed to God was "pleasant to the sight" (Genesis 2:9) and was not "enticing to the eyes" (Genesis 3:6), illustrates the fact that God was not responsible for the presence of the forbidden tree. Recalling that "eating" can indicate "understanding," consider James 1:5-6 where is written,

> "If any of you lacks wisdom, let him ask of God, WHO GIVES TO ALL LIBERALLY AND WITHOUT REPROACH, and IT WILL BE GIVEN TO HIM; but let him ask in faith, with no doubting, for he who doubts is like a wave of the sea driven and tossed by the wind."

The notion that God created the forbidden tree casts doubt onto our perceptions of Him. According to James 1:5-6, to state that God restricted humanity from wisdom on account of the forbidden tree is a blatant contradiction if God is willing to give "wisdom" to "all" and in a manner that is "without" reproach. Furthermore, we know that the letter ב was understood as both a "womb" and "wisdom," and we may consider that we have already seen that "fruit" can be used in the sense of the product of the womb. Peculiarly, the Hebrew letters that we render "השכיל to make one wise" in Genesis 3:6 regarding "the tree" can also mean to bereave one of children and "השכיל to cause to miscarry, to suffer abortion" (chiefly depending on the sibilant). That is, the root שכל, if pronounced "sacal" means to make wise, but if it is pronounced "shacole" means to miscarry, to suffer abortion. The Hebrew word for רע evil used in the Eden narrative of Genesis 2-3 is the word for רע injury. Knowing that "vines" were understood as "trees" in the Hebrew Scriptures helps us to understand a Tree of the Knowledge of Good and רע Evil [or רע injury], for when we consider the commonality of poisonous vines, we should also consider the fact that abortions are committed in Eastern Africa today by consuming poison. To the scribes of Scripture, consumable wine, that is, wine that was mixed with 2/3 water, was called "fruit of the vine"; wine that was not fit for consumption, that is, wine that was unmixed with water, was called "fruit of the tree," i.e. the fruit of the (vine-) tree (consult Lightfoot's *Commentary on the New Testament from the Talmud and Hebraica*; Vol. 2, p. 351); we have an indication of this when Christ specifically said that,

> "I tell you, I will never again drink of this FRUIT OF THE VINE until that day when I drink it new with you in My Father's Kingdom," (Matthew 26:29);

but then we read,

> "A jar full of SOUR WINE was standing there. So they put a sponge full of the wine on a branch of hyssop and held it to His mouth. When Jesus had RECEIVED THE WINE, He said, 'It is finished.' Then He bowed his head and died," (John 19:29-30).

Christ consumed the "fruit of the tree" as He hung on the "tree" — He did not receive the "fruit of the vine" on the cross. However, when, "...one of the soldiers pierced His side with a spear, and at once blood AND WATER came out," (John 19:34), we may understand that the "fruit of the vine" flowed out of Christ in accordance with His New Covenant and in relation to the fact that He called Himself the "True Vine" in John 15:1, for the Torah calls wine the "blood of the grape" in Genesis 49:11 and Deuteronomy 32:14. Furthermore, "blood" was not to be "eaten" (Leviticus 3:17; 7:26,27; 17:10,12,14; 19:26), and "eating" blood was understood as "drinking" blood (Leviticus 23:24). We may therefore understand the figure: "eating" the "fruit of the tree" is the same as drinking forbidden wine or consuming forbidden blood or eating the forbidden "fruit of the tree." Since the "destruction" of someone was as the consumption or "eating" of someone (Numbers 16:45), since "eating" also indicated acquiring *knowledge*, since "blood" was called "life" by the Torah (Leviticus 17:14), and since the marital union was understood as "*knowing*," we can understand that eating the forbidden fruit of the Tree of the *Knowledge*... meant the eventual destruction of life... hence, the Hebrew letters that we render "השכיל *to make one wise*" in Genesis 3:6 regarding "the tree" can also mean *to bereave one of children* and "השכיל *to cause to miscarry, to suffer abortion*."

Consider the Hebrew relation of "burning" and "consuming," that is, "eating." Even during the time of Pliny, human sacrifice was understood as "*eating* human flesh" because such sacrificed human flesh was *burnt* (*Natural History*, Book VII; Pliny), and such imagery can be observed Scripturally:

> "Please do not let her be as one dead, whose flesh is half CONSUMED when he comes out of the womb of אמנו *our mother*," (Numbers 12;12).

That a human sacrifice plunged the world into ruin necessitated that a Human sacrifice redeem the world from ruin... "because it is impossible for the blood of bulls and goats to take away sins," and animal sacrifice was but a "reminder" of human error (Hebrews 10:3-4). The Enemy deceived the woman into sacrificing the son of Adam accidentally through manslaughter, whereas Satan was a "murderer from the beginning," (John 8:44). Exodus 22:5 discusses livestock that "בער *burn* in another man's field," and the next verse discusses a fire that "אכל *eats*" grain. It would, at first, appear that livestock "eat" and that fire "burns," but the Torah states that livestock "burn" and fire "eats"; the logic of the juxtaposition of "burning" and "eating" is apparent, for "burning" and "eating" were both understood in the sense of consumption... hence the referential description of the baby who had "*half-eaten flesh*" in Numbers 12:12. Even the Romans during the time of Christ understood that the sacrifice of a human was compared to cannibalism, that is, the "burning" or "sacrificing" of human flesh was compared to the metaphorical "eating" of human flesh (for an altar is a table).

Since God's punishments fit crimes perfectly, we can understand why, when Adam and his wife ate the fruit of the tree, their life was then required of them according to God's Word (Genesis 2:17), though not immediately, which is another indication that they did not intend to kill their child in the womb, for they were banished from the garden rather than slain in the garden, as such a situation was eventually encapsulated within the laws pertaining to the cities of refuge (Numbers 35) marked out for manslayers, not murderers. The *Babylonian Talmud's* "Pesahim" warns pregnant women regarding various alcoholic beverages — in our thematic case, what the Hebrews called the "fruit of the tree"; furthermore, even the writers of the *Talmud* knew that that the forbidden tree was a grapevine (in *Talmud*: "Sanhedrin"), and since the expression "fruit of the tree" meant wine unmixed with water (as opposed to the expression "fruit of the vine"), the Talmudists believe that Adam was drunk and thus fell into sin. It was not thought that alcohol was inherently sinful to the people in Biblical times (lest we claim that Christ's miracle involving wine in the Book of John was sinful... along with Holy Communion, or unless we admit the fabulous doctrine that "wine" somehow means "grape-juice" — despite the diction of Scripture), but that wine had to be proportionately diluted and was not to be used in overindulgence. The point expressed here does not concern alcohol consumption, but rather the consumption of toxins that lead to death by poisoning.

> "Do you not know this of old, since ADAM was placed on earth, that the triumphing of the wicked is short, and the joy of the hypocrite is but for a moment?

Though his haughtiness mounts up to the heavens, and his head reaches to the clouds, yet he will perish forever like his own refuse; those who have seen him will say, 'Where is he?' He will fly away like a dream, and not be found; yes, he will be chased away like a vision of the night. The eye that saw him will see him no more, nor will his place behold him anymore. His children will seek the favor of the poor, and his hands will restore his wealth. His bones are full of his youthful vigor, but it will lie down with him in the dust. THOUGH EVIL IS SWEET IN HIS MOUTH, and he hides it under his tongue, though he spares it and does not forsake it, but still keeps it in his mouth, yet his food in his stomach turns SOUR; IT BECOMES COBRA VENOM within him. He swallows down riches and vomits them up again; God casts them out of his belly. He will suck the POISON OF COBRAS; the VIPER'S TONGUE will slay him," (Job 20:4-16).

We may grasp the parallel between cobra poison and toxic words, for the Apostle Paul utilized the same imagery by quotation in Romans 3:13-17.

The forbidden tree had to be a poisonous vine for many reasons, one of which is that, since the great Fall of Man Narrative deals with the so-called "serpent," poison and drunkenness (or something like them) must have been a part of the Fall, for "eating" words meant "making words part of oneself." That is, some Arabian snakes infect with neurotoxin (nerve-affecting venom), and such venom causes a victim to appear to be drunk, for his eyelids become heavy, his pupils dilate, he becomes incoherent, he is unable to balance himself, and he is unable to speak properly... and such a reference was made by King Solomon:

"Who has DULLNESS OF EYES? — those who stay long

at the wine; those who go to seek mixed wine. Do not look at wine when it is red, when it sparkles in the cup and goes down smoothly. At last it BITES LIKE THE SERPENT and STINGS LIKE THE ADDER. Your eyes will see strange things, and your mind utter perverse things. You will be like one who lies down in the midst of the sea, like one who lies on top of a mast [that is, swaying and UNABLE TO KEEP BALANCE]," (Proverbs 23:29-34).

Again, the forbidden tree had to be a poisonous vine for many reasons. Since the great Fall of Man Narrative deals with the so-called "serpent," poison and drunkenness (or something like them) must have been a part of the Fall, for "eating" poisonous words meant "making poison part of oneself." Consider the grim parallel in the Noah Narrative. However, the "drunkenness" under discussion is not aimed at claiming that Adam had a vineyard from which he fermented wine and became intoxicated (whether he did or not may be studied at length in another book), but rather that, thematically, his lack of proper judgment effected deadly results that align seamlessly with the effects of venomous serpents. The "venom" under discussion is not aimed at claiming that the first humans were actually bitten by a literal snake, but rather that, thematically, the taint of sin is suitably paralleled to serpentine poison and drunkenness, that is, lack of discretion. Davidson's *Analytical Hebrew and Chaldee Lexicon* defines the Scriptural, feminine noun חידה as *enigma, proverb, parable*; hence *sublime, spiritual discourse*; this word also means *riddle* (as in Numbers 12:8); it is from the root חוד *to tie* and the Rev. S. C. Malan, D.D., Late Vicar of Broadwindsor, Dorset's work on the Book of *Proverbs* defines חידה *riddle* as a *twisted* [*woven*]*, tangled saying* (p. 19); consider a vine *interlacing* the branches of a tree. That "wisdom" was a part of the Narrative regarding a forbidden (vine-) tree in Eden illustrates a perfect parallel to the word חידה *riddle,* which can indicate something *woven, tangled,* and therefore *interlaced...* as is true of a vine upon a tree, stake, or trellis... like snakes in trees, as were so common when Scripture was written, it need not even be elaborated upon.

Specifically, the words "fruit of the tree" were *not* spoken by God, Adam, or Satan in the Eden Narrative, but only by the woman. "Fruit of the tree" was an expression. "Fruit of the tree" indicated wine unmixed with water. I do not mean to assert dogmatically that our first parents actually drank something in the great Fall (whether they did or not, I do not know); rather, that the fruit (or liquid from it) that they consumed is perfectly paralleled to the expression "fruit of the tree" that was commonly understood in the days of Moses. Accordingly, even well over a thousand years later, Pliny's thirteenth book of Natural History discussed a plant known as the "snake-vine" that is "injurious to the womb" (consider Genesis 3:16) and that "produces vomiting" (consider Job 20). In Hebrew, the word אשכל *grape-cluster* comes from the root שכל *to lose children, to become childless, to miscarry, to suffer abortion.* Pliny's fourteenth book of Natural History states,

> "Similarly in Thasos also hellebore is planted among the vines, or else wild cucumber or scammony; the wine so obtained is called by a Greek name denoting miscarriage, because it produces abortion."

In the same volume, Pliny wrote,

> "Egypt also possess a wine called in Greek 'delivery wine' which causes abortion."

People in Greece and Egypt (where Moses was born and raised) used the "fruit of the tree" to kill their children in the womb; hence, when Moses penned the words "fruit of the tree," the expression, though difficult (if not impossible) to be understood out of context, made perfect sense if one knew the context — for the very first command given to humanity was to be "fruitful," and the very first prohibition was called "fruit of the tree" by the *woman* and none other. When we consider the (snake-) vine (the forbidden tree) on the Tree of Life, we may note that Pliny's seventeenth book of Natural History states a practice that resembles staffs turning into serpents:

> "A plan has recently been invented of planting a SNAKE-BRANCH near the tree — that is our name for a veteran main branch that has grown hard with many years' service. The quickest plan in the case of A VINE is to cut this old branch off as long as possible and scrape the bark off three-quarters of its length, down to the point to which it is to be buried in the ground — for this reason it is also called a 'scraped' shoot — and then to press it down in the furrow, with the remaining part STANDING STRAIGHT UP AGAINST THE TREE."

Here, we have a suitable parallel as to how, perhaps, the Enemy penetrated Eden and planted his shaft upon the strength of the central tree, for the "recent" plan discussed in the quotation above was probably only recent to the Romans when Pliny was writing (shortly after the ascension of Christ), for it certainly existed before there was a Rome; nevertheless, here we have yet another instance where secular natural history attests to the veracity of Holy Writ unawares. Vines resemble snakes in many ways, and the thematic link between these two entities requires no stretch of the imagination. Since both a vine's product and a snake's venom produce similar outward effects, it is evident why the Eden Narrative would utilize the imagery of a deadly "serpent" in conjunction with a deadly "tree" (a "vine-tree"), for the results of neurotoxin and intoxication appear outwardly similar, and thus the

Narrative's figuration would have been more potent to its initial readers within their own geography than with us within our geography today. Even the Talmudists knew that the forbidden tree was a vine (*Talmud*: "Sanhedrin"). The very fact that a riddle had been propounded by the serpentine enemy indicated (figuratively) that a knot had been tied (חוד), a strand had been TANGLED (חידה), a vine had INTERLACED itself upon a trellis, a snake had WOVEN itself in the branches of a tree... In his seventeenth book of *Natural History*, Pliny wrote that "When a vine has become hard, it is very bad to bring it across on a trellis. When a vine is four years old the main branches themselves are TWISTED over, and each throws out one growth of wood, first one and then the next ones, and the earlier shoots are pruned away." The relation of a snake to a vine is perfect, and such relational imagery is entirely lost if the reader reads the word "tree" as merely a tree according to the English language (which was not in existence when Moses wrote). In other words, the Narrative of the Fall explains faulty reasoning and the deadly consequences that result from a lack of wisdom; since both neurotoxin and intoxication can render one unable to speak properly, Scripture illustrates the woman's misquotations (Genesis 3:2-3). Since both neurotoxin and intoxication make the eyelids heavy, the "serpent" said "...your eyes shall be opened..." (Genesis 3:5; compare to Genesis 3:7), and knowing that the venom under discussion dilates the pupils, we may observe the parallel fact that dilated pupils facilitate night vision and can make beholding light painful; utilizing such a physical fact as an illustration of morality, we may also observe the following:

> "And this is the condemnation, that the light has come into the world, and men loved darkness rather than light, because their deeds were evil. For everyone practicing evil hates the light and does not come to

the light, lest his deeds should be exposed. But he who does the truth comes to the light, that his deeds may be clearly seen, that they have been done in God," (John 3:19-21).

Since neurotoxin causes an inability to balance, such causation fits the great *Fall* of MAN Narrative, as does the fact that grapes are gathered in the time of death (Autumn) as opposed to "The Time of Life" (Genesis 18:14), which, being translated, means "the Spring season." In perfect parallel to a snake-bite that can cause maladies that mimic drunkenness, the idea of one partaking of a poisonous vine, the "fruit of the tree," compares inebriation to self-poisoning; that is, the Eden account discusses poor decision-making and its dire consequences, i.e. departing from the Living God, with a preference for the one who has the power of death, through errant choices and lack of wise judgment. The Eden story is an account of a "serpent" that charmed people instead of people who charmed a serpent. Consider the dominion of a riddler. "If a snake bites before it is charmed, there is no profit for the *master of the tongue* [the "*lord of the language,*" the "*charmer*"]," (Ecclesiastes 10:11); in other words, as the word משל can mean *to rule* and *to riddle*, the word בעל *master, lord* comes from the root בעל *to have dominion*. The charmer rules over the charmed. *To rule* and *to riddle* are the same Hebrew word (משל), and the word חידה *riddle* comes from the root חוד *to tie*; notice that Christ called Satan the "prince of this world" just before Christ identified Himself as the "True Vine" (John 14:30-15:1), for the false, twisted vine, the forbidden tree, illustrated the Enemy. Consider the juxtaposition of snakes and vines:

> "In that day the Lord with His severe sword, great and strong, will punish Leviathan the fleeing serpent, Leviathan that TWISTED serpent; and He will

> slay the reptile that is in the sea. In that day sing to
> her, 'A VINEYARD of red wine!'" (Isaiah 27:1-2).

In order to understand the forbidden tree, it is imperative
to understand venomous snakes. The forbidden tree must
have been a poisonous vine, for the facts that vines resemble
snakes, that Scripture continually compares vines to snakes,
that both vines and snakes produce their own kinds of drunkenness (so to speak), and that the woman did not speak
properly all indicate that the forbidden tree (in conjunction
with the "serpent") must have been a deadly vine. The deception that the woman accepted killed the firstborn of humanity which is why להשכיל spells *to make one wise* and *to
cause miscarriage, to cause abortion* in an unpointed Text
of Genesis 3:6, for (again) the consumption of poison is still
a method of abortion utilized today. Consider a man being
"bound" and his "house" being plundered. A womb was often
described as a "basin" or some concave vessel (like a threshold) in antiquity. By Satan's deception, Adam's wife deliberately ate the forbidden fruit, but accidentally miscarried on
account of her ignorance and rebellion. The noun נחש *serpent*
in Genesis 3 is spelled exactly the same (in an unpointed
Text) as the verb נחש *to divine*, that is, the divination by cups
or basins described in Genesis 44:5 (and this word can also
indicate divination by serpents); the word בטן is rendered (1)
bowl in I Kings 7:20, (2) *belly* in Numbers 5:22, and (3) *womb*
in Genesis 25:23. Therefore, consuming the fruit of the tree
was the same as destroying the life in the basin, i.e. killing the
fruit of the womb, which reflects the reason why blood was
taken from the סף *basin, threshold* in preparation for the first
Passover when the firstborn sons of the Egyptians were slain.
Note that Song of Songs 7:3 refers to a woman's navel as
a אגן *goblet,* a *cup,* and consider how offspring is compared
to האגנות *the bowls* in Isaiah 22:24. The snake and the vine
are perfect illustrations of what happened in Eden, and to

cancel such a fatal error, Christ (antithetically) became as a "serpent" (John 3:14) and the True Vine (John 15:1); Christ died on a tree on account of poison (John 19:28-30) which killed much more quickly than a typical crucifixion, which is why Pilate was "surprised" (Mark 15:44) that Jesus died as soon as He did.

When considering that the very first command given to humanity was to "be fruitful and multiply," when reflecting on words like "garden" and "rivers," when recalling rivers and lands with procreative names in the Eden Narrative, when considering "seed," "wisdom," etc., why would we not consider the fact that the woman was pregnant when she ate of the forbidden tree when a word signifying "abortion" is present in the very story of life versus death? The forbidden tree could not have been planted by God, nor could it have held wisdom. The Enemy must have planted the forbidden, injurious tree by manipulating God's creation in a similar manner to the way in which seedless grapes are produced today. The forbidden tree was the opposite of the Tree of Life; it was a tree of death. The forbidden tree could not "make one wise"; it, instead, "bereaved one of children" and "caused abortion." The forbidden, seedless grapevine made the first humans seedless, that is, naked, that is, childless. Knowing that God's punishments fit crimes perfectly, and that God's grace fits His punishments perfectly, we can therefore understand why He said,

> "...I will greatly multiply your sorrow and your conception; IN PAIN YOU SHALL BRING FORTH CHILDREN..." (Genesis 3:16).

Consider: "If I COVERED my transgressions as Adam..." (Job 31:33); Adam was a gardener. Adam knew how to dig. Since, without question, a corpse that was buried in soil was understood to defile the ground (which is why the Hebrews did not bury people under soil), there is no other reason besides the fact that Adam buried his infant son's corpse in the soil that God said,

> "...CURSED is the GROUND for your sake; in toil you shall EAT of it all the days of your life," (Genesis 3:17).

Since God is perfectly just, we can see why He cursed the ground, since something dead was buried within it. Furthermore, innocently shed blood was said to "pollute" the land (Numbers 35:33); in other words, innocently shed blood caused the ground to become accursed. Knowing that the river "*Gihon*" means "*Belly, as the source of the fetus,*" we can see why God, in His perfect justice, said to the "serpent,"

> "...On your *belly* [from the root "*gahon*"] you shall go and you shall eat dust all the days of your life. And I will put enmity between you and the woman, and between your seed and her Seed..." (Genesis 3:14-15).

The words "belly," and "the source of the fetus" are certainly a wordplay, for before the insertion of the vowel letters and the vowel points into the Hebrew Scriptures, the words "Gihon (Belly, as the source of the fetus)" and "belly" were probably spelled identically, and this helps explain why *Strong's Exhaustive Concordance* links the word "belly (gahon)" to the river "Gihon (Source of the Fetus)." Furthermore, "Gihon" and "belly" are spelled with the exact same consonants between Genesis 3:14 and I Kings 1:33. That is, since God gave humanity the Tree of Life, Satan gave humanity the tree of death. Since God told people to be "fruitful," Satan deceived the woman into consuming the "fruit" of her womb by consuming *the fruit of the tree (venom, drunkenness,* that is *poor and wicked decision-making)*, hence God's pronouncement of enmity that He would place between the "seed" of Satan and the "Seed" of the woman. Since paradises housed gardens, and since a garden can be turned into a paradise through impregnation, it is no wonder that "Eden," which indicates the "womb," was only called a "garden" and not a "paradise" in the Genesis 2-3 narrative, for the firstborn of humanity, the son of Adam, was birthed a disfigured corpse on account of the forbidden tree, as it is written in the Hebrew Text,

> "Please do not let her be as one dead, whose flesh is half consumed when he comes out of the womb of אמנו *our mother*," (Numbers 12;12), that is, our mother Eve (see Ginsburg's *Introduction to the Massoretico-Critical Edition of the Hebrew Bible, p. 348*).

The quotation above explains why it was only after the woman sinned that Adam then named his wife חוה *Life* because היתה *she became* the mother of all the living (Genesis 3:20), for she began as the mother of the dead.

When Genesis was first written, infants who died (probably under the age of 30 days) did not have their names remembered (hence the general understanding recorded in Ecclesiastes 6:4) but, if and when they were referred to (and if they were males), they were simply called the "son" of their father; and this explains why Christ continually referred to Himself as "The Son of Adam/Man," and why He is called "The Firstborn of the Dead" in Colossians 1:18 and Revelation 1:5. God's punishment fit the crime, and His grace fits the punishment; therefore, the son of Adam died on account of a tree and thus the earth was doomed... so God came down as "The Son of Adam" (The Son of Man) and died on a tree in order to save the world from doom. Satan enticed the woman into "eating" from the forbidden tree; she "consumed" the "fruit" of her womb; since the woman was the only one in Genesis 2-3 who mentioned fruit ("fruit of the tree"), then we can understand James 1:14-16:

> "...one is tempted by ONE'S OWN DESIRE, being lured and enticed by it; then, when that desire has CONCEIVED, it gives birth to sin, and that sin, when it is fully grown, GIVES BIRTH to DEATH," (James 1:14-15).

I Timothy 2:14 states that

> "...Adam was not deceived, but the woman being deceived, fell into transgression."

Baal-zebub (Satan) is called the "god of Ekron" in II Kings 1:1-4. In Matthew 12:24, this grim title is rendered "Baal-zebul" in Greek which can mean "lord of abominable idols, prince of idols and idolatry" i.e. the chief of all wickedness. "Ekron" was a Philistine city, and "Ekron" is derived from the same root as the adjective "barren" that is employed to explain childless people, who were made childless in one manner or another. It would stand to reason that chief of all wickedness, Baal-zebub of Ekron, is none other than Satan, the god of barrenness who opposes the "Living God." That is, it seems as if the manner in which "Ekron" is spelled was devised to associate barrenness with Satan (Zephaniah 2:4). The battle is between Life and Death, God and Satan; thus, one can reflect on all the principle women in Scripture who had tremendous difficulty in becoming pregnant in successive connection to the prophesied Messiah. It is markedly evident that Satan, the "god of *Ekron*," who is the god of *barrenness*, was focused on uprooting a family line in order to subvert the prophecy pronounced by God in Eden. Ironically, Mary not only had ease in becoming pregnant, but did not even have to lift a finger to do so, and one may behold such an exclamation-point in enraptured awe in light of the fact that countless women were made childless by Herod on account of Christ's birth. When one reflects on the fact that Ahaziah "fell" and injured himself, sought the word of Baal-zebub, the god of Ekron, and was told through the Angel of the Lord's message to Elijah that he would "surely die" for having sought Satan in II Kings 1:1-4, we must be looking at a direct parallel to the words of Satan, the Fall of Man, and the condemnation of certain death that occurred in Eden.

As we have already grasped that the letter ב, the "house," was understood as signifying both a "womb" and "wisdom," we can understand more of why the letters שכל can be pronounced to signify abortion/miscarriage or wisdom (chiefly depending on the sibilant). Earlier, I asked, "How can 'Life' indicate something fallen?" regarding the fact that "Life" was the name given to Adam's wife in her fallen state. When we discuss the great "Fall" of humanity, it has been forgotten that this "Fall" indicates "abortion" literally. The noun נפל means *an abortion*, and it comes from the root נפל *to fall*. When Adam and his wife accidentally aborted their firstborn, the נפל *Fall*, that is, the *Abortion* occurred; this was supposed to have been remembered by the construction the Holy ארון *coffin* that we call the Holy "Ark," for the word ארון *ark* means *a coffin* (Genesis 50:26) and the *Babylonian Talmud's* "Sotah" preserves this fact as well; this coffin (the Holy Ark) had cherubs at either end of its propitiation slab or atonement cover (that is called the "mercy seat"), upon which the atonement blood was to be placed... and since the Jews did not have the ark during the earthly days of Christ, the foundation-stone received the blood instead. Since Christ was whipped before He died and was laid in a stone tomb after He died, His blood touched the slab of stone (in the womb/the cave), and the reader will notice that the cherubs were positioned on either end of the stone slab (John 20:10-12) just as they were atop the holy ark, the holy coffin (which was constructed of dimensions fit for a child's elaborate, ornate, royal coffin), especially when considering ancient Persia, the home of the Magi. That is, the ancient Persians did not allow a corpse to mingle with soil (since a corpse defiled, or cursed, the soil), and when a king died, they placed his lifeless clay into a golden coffin that was covered with a tight-fitting lid; this ark was placed within a mausoleum (house/temple/womb), and the building was built in a garden that was protected by priestly guards like the cherubs that were set to "guard the way of the Tree of Life" (Genesis 3:24) following the death of Adam's heir. Furthermore, since the unvowelized verb שכל can be rendered *to be wise* and also *to suffer abortion/bereave of children*, we cannot avoid thinking of Christ (in thematic inverse) when Genesis 48:14 uses this verb to describe a *cross (i.e. to cross; the crossing of hands).*

Please allow me to repeat myself in order to assert a point:

We must remember that God "built" the woman in Genesis 2:22 as a wise master builder builds a house... as One builds a family... and we must also remember that when the "House of God" is mentioned in Scripture, the Text refers to His Temple; God's first official Temple that was constructed by human hands was the Tabernacle. Followers of Christ are the bride of Christ (II Corinthians 11:2), and it stands to reason why the bride of Christ is also His "body" (Ephesians 5:22-24) and his "temple" because "God's Spirit lives within" His followers (I Corinthians 3:16). Such imagery can be understood more clearly when we read how the act of slaying one's own child ("seed") defiles God's "sanctuary" (Leviticus 20:3) since this sanctuary is the womb. A "father's nakedness" or "father's skirt" refers to a man's mother, step-mother, or the concubine of a man's father (Genesis 9:22; Leviticus 20:11; Deuteronomy 27:20; Ezekiel 22:10); that is, *a man's nakedness* can refer to *his bride's flesh*, and *a bride's nakedness* can refer to *her husband's flesh*:

"The man who lies with HIS FATHER'S WIFE has uncovered HIS FATHER'S NAKEDNESS; both of them shall surely be put to death. Their blood shall be upon them," (Leviticus 20:11).

The "sanctuary" is in the "bride," just as God "built" the woman (like a house) in Genesis 2:22. Consider that God's house, the tabernacle in the wilderness, had a bridal train that hung from the rear of it (Exodus 26:12) and was led throughout the wilderness, like a royal marriage procession, by a "pillar of cloud by day" (Numbers 14:14). It is also helpful to think of a אפריון *palanquin (an East Asian* COVERED *litter,* CARRIED ON POLES *on the shoulders of two or* FOUR *men; a bed).*

"Who is this coming out of the WILDERNESS like PILLARS OF SMOKE, perfumed with myrrh and frankincense, with all the merchant's fragrant powders? Behold, it is Solomon's couch, with sixty valiant men around it, of the valiant of Israel. They all hold swords, being expert in war. Every man has his sword on his thigh because of fear in the night. Of the wood of Lebanon Solomon the King made himself a *palanquin [like the Holy Ark with its poles]:* he made its pillars of silver, its support of gold, its seat of purple, its interior paved with love by the daughters of Jerusalem. Go forth, O daughters of Zion, and see King Solomon with the crown with which his mother crowned him on the day of his WEDDING, the day of the gladness of his heart," (Song of Songs 3:6-11).

II Chronicles 16:4 provides a blatant parallel between death and sleep in that the "bed" in this passage was that of the tomb. Again, regarding the palanquin discussed above, Ginsburg wrote, "Palanquins were and are still used in the

East by great personages. They are like a couch, sufficiently long for the rider to recline, covered with a canopy resting on pillars at the four corners, hung round with curtains to exclude the sun; they have a door, sometimes a lattice-work on each side. They are borne by four or more men, by means of strong poles," (p. 152). The word אפריון *palanquin* (rendered "chariot," and "bed") is derived from the root פרה *to be fruitful*, hence its bed-like construction. The first command given to humanity was to "be fruitful" (Genesis 1:28). The holy ארון *ark* is from the root ארה *to gather*, and this root produces the Hebrew words "stall," "stable," and "lion," and we may note the humble conditions that Jesus was born under, along with the fact that He is the "Lion of the Tribe of Judah" (Revelation 5:5), whose tomb was situated like the foundation stone in the Temple where the Ark, the holy coffin, was supposed to be; the slab that Christ's body was laid upon was fit for The Son of Adam, and the propitiation slab atop the holy coffin, the Ark, was fit for an infant (the son of Adam). As palanquins had lattice-work on each side, we may reflect on the crown that surrounded the Ark (Exodus 25:11), and we may reflect on the fact that Christ, the King, wore a crown of thorns like the curse of Genesis 3:18. Palanquins were supported by poles, as was true of the Ark (Exodus 25:14), as Christ, the "True Vine" (John 15:1), was when He died. In the same way that many did not believe in Him when He hung on the cross, so many did not believe Joshua (Jesus) when he returned from scouting out the promised land, as he was accompanied by a grape-cluster that hung on a pole between those who carried it; אשכל *grape-cluster* comes from the root שכל *to lose children, to become childless, to miscarry, to suffer abortion*. Palanquins were covered by a canopy, and the top of the Ark was covered by the wings of the cherubs (Exodus 25:20), like the situation of the angels in Christ's tomb (John 20:10-12). Palanquins were like chariots, the Ark was known as a chariot (I Chronicles 28:18), and Christ traveled back from the dead within His tomb. God filled the craftsmen of His Tabernacle with חכמה *wisdom* (Exodus 31:3-5) and when we consider its synonym שכל *wisdom*, we may reflect on the fact that this unpointed word, depending on the context under which it is employed, can signify *miscarriage* and *abortion*; similarly, Adam's wife was to bring forth fruit by Adam's support ("palanquin" comes from the root "to be fruitful"), and we can see how her womb became the son of Adam's grave (the Hebrew word for the Holy "Ark" means a "coffin") like the words of Job 3 and Jeremiah 20:17: "...or that my mother might have been my grave..." The Tabernacle, that was "built" up like Adam's wife, was led forth in a quasi-marital procession (that is, walking in covenant), and its Holy of Holies (its womb) held the coffin of the royal infant (and inside the coffin were symbols of the heir of Adam, the son of Man, The Heir of Adam, The Son of Man); in triumph, the Living God spoke from on top of the coffin like One Who crushed death underfoot as was prophesied in Genesis 3:15 and as was accomplished in Christ's tomb that had been foreshadowed by the design of the Tabernacle. For whatever reason, Joseph's coffin (Genesis 50:26) is often but remembered as a coffin, and the Holy Ark is often but remembered as a box — but both Joseph's "coffin" and the Holy "Ark" are the same Hebrew word; therefore, one could justly recall Joseph's "ark" and the Holy "coffin" when referring to these two boxes. The "Ark" and "coffin" are both understood as beds, hence the importance of a palanquin, a litter; II Chronicles 16:4 provides a blatant parallel between death and sleep in that the "bed" in this passage was that of the tomb. It is amazing to consider that, today, scientists are describing the womb as a "book" because they are discovering pre-determined information written within it... and though this description of a womb/book is an amazing discovery, it is by no means new.

Consider the Book of the Torah and the "appointed times (the feasts)" of Israel (Leviticus 23), for the word "feast" comes from the root יעד *to betroth*, and to remember the son of Adam, the annual circuit of the feasts was set to mirror human gestation (refer to Zola Levit's wonderful and underrated work called "The Seven Feasts of Israel"). That is, the average pregnancy lasts for about 280 days. The true Torah New Year is the first day of the month in which פסח *Passover* occurs (Exodus 12:2), and the root of the word "Hebrew" is עבר *to pass over*, i.e. into covenant with God, as is true in proper marriage. The feasts (*appointed times*) begin in the spring season that Scripture calls "The Time of Life" (Genesis 18:14). If we consider an ideal Hebrew year (one that begins on the spring equinox) in light of the duration of a pregnancy, then a typical pregnancy beginning on the spring equinox (on the "time of life") would result in a birth on Christmas. The egg appears on the 14th day of the first month (Passover). The sowing of man's seed must occur within 24 hours (Unleavened Bread). The fertilized egg implants within two to six days (First Fruits). Sticking to an average of 50 days from fertilization (accounting for the variables between one mother and the next), at this point the embryo displays markedly human characteristics (Pentecost). On the first day of the seventh month, the tiny human's hearing capacity develops (the Feast of Trumpets). On the 10th day of the seventh month (Atonement), the hemoglobin of the blood changes from that of a fetus to that of a self-sustaining human. On the 15th day of the seventh month, a baby is equipped with two healthy lungs (Tabernacles). In other words, the very dates that the Torah mandates for the feasts of Israel are distinctly patterned to reflect the development of a child in the womb *from the point of conception*, and if the reader refers to each feast in the Torah, he will discover that the dates of gestation mentioned above are the dates of the feasts of Israel. Let us conclude this point by reflecting on the fact that the Torah has 613 total laws made up of **248** positive laws and **365** negative laws. Ephesians 2 says that the "enmity" of Genesis 3:15 is the Torah (**248**+**365**=613), for the number of the Torah's laws is set to preserve the history of the abortion in the garden = the destroyer in the womb.

I now appeal to those familiar with Gematria:

(א) = 1	(י) = 10	(ק) = 100
(ב) = 2	(כ) = 20	(ר) = 200
(ג) = 3	(ל) = 30	(שׁ) = 300
(ד) = 4	(מ) = 40	(ת) = 400
(ה) = 5	(נ) = 50	(ך) = 500 or 20
(ו) = 6	(ס) = 60	(ם) = 600 or 40
(ז) = 7	(ע) = 70	(ן) = 700 or 50
(ח) = 8	(פ) = 80	(ף) = 800 or 80
(ט) = 9	(צ) = 90	(ץ) = 900 or 90

(α) = 1	(ι) = 10	(ρ) = 100
(β) = 2	(κ) = 20	(σ) = 200 or 6
(γ) = 3	(λ) = 30	(τ) = 300
(δ) = 4	(μ) = 40	(υ) = 400
(ε) = 5	(ν) = 50	(φ) = 500
(ς) = 6	(ξ) = 60	(χ) = 600
(ζ) = 7	(ο) = 70	(ψ) =700
(η) = 8	(π) = 80	(ω) = 800
(θ) = 9	Koppa = 90	(ϡ) = 900

שסה *destroyer* = ש+ס+ה = 300+60+5 = **365**
עצרה *assembly* (from עצר *to rule*; consider עצר *restraining the womb from childbearing*) = ע+צ+ר+ה = 5+70+90+200 = **365**
Σατανας *Satan* = "Σ+α+τ+α+ν+α+ς" = 6+1+300+1+50+1+6= **365**.

רחם *womb* = ם+ח+ר = 40+8+200 = **248**
רחם *to love* = ם+ח+ר = 40+8+200 = **248**
מרח *to crush, to bruise* = ח+ר+מ = 8+200+40 = **248**

Again, Ephesians 2 says that the "enmity" of Genesis 3:15 (placed between the *woman* and the "serpent") is the Torah (**248+365** = 613); consider the gematria of the synonyms above within the quotation below:

> "The Lord said to the נחש *serpent* [Σατανας, שׂטה = **365**]... 'I will put **enmity** [**365+248**= TORAH] between you and the woman, and between your seed and her Seed; ישׁפך *He shall bruise* [מרח = **248**] your head, and תשׁופנו *you shall bruise* [מרח = **248**] His heel.' To the woman He said: 'I will greatly multiply your sorrow והרנך *and your conception* [רחם = **248**]; in pain תלדי *you shall bring forth children* [רחם = **248**]; your desire shall be for your husband, and ימשׁל *he shall rule* [עצר → עצרה = **365**] over you,'" (Genesis 3:14-16).

However, an in-depth study of the Torah Laws and the Ark as revealed above is the substance of another book and another time. Glory belongs to God in the Highest! — and I pray that He allows me the honor of writing such a study, in another book, with the thorough, patient, and delicate respect such a study deserves. For now, let it be known that the Torah conceals the blueprint of human life itself; that is, the structure of the Torah (its order, its festivals, the components of the tabernacle, etc.) perfectly mirrors the development of a human baby in the womb, which is why the festivals were set with such precision. The Torah was written in a time when no human knew, by science, specifically *how* a child develops in the womb. Since the structure of the Torah mirrors gestation, and since the Torah was written in an era that predates the scientific discovery of the intricate processes of gestation, the Torah could not possibly have been designed by a mere human [note 7, p. 173], though it was penned by human hands in the manner of a King (a Ruler = a Riddler) and His royal scribe.

Let us reflect upon the Menorah, the Tree of Life. The seven fires of the Menorah represent the Seven Spirits of God, as explained in Revelation 4:5: "...Seven lamps of fire were burning before the throne, which are the seven Spirits of God." Is it not concerning the Tree of Life and infant son of Adam in relation to Christ that this is written in the 11th chapter of Isaiah (?):

> "There shall come forth a Rod from the stem of Jesse, and a Branch shall grow out of his roots. The Spirit of [1] the Lord shall rest upon Him, the Spirit of [2] wisdom and [3] understanding, the Spirit of [4] counsel and [5] might, the Spirit of [6] knowledge and of the [7] fear of the Lord..."

Notice that the Spirit of *wisdom* is the *second* spirit, the ב spirit, for the number 2 is the letter ב *house = womb = wisdom,* as we have already seen clearly with particular reference to the *second* river from Eden that Is called גיחון *Belly, as the Source of the Fetus* in Genesis 2:13. Isaiah continues:

> "...His delight is in the fear of the Lord, And He shall not judge by the sight of His eyes, nor decide by the hearing of His ears; but with righteousness He shall judge the poor, and decide with equity for the meek of the earth; He shall strike the earth with the rod of His mouth, and with the breath of His lips He shall slay the wicked. Righteousness shall be the belt of His loins, and faithfulness the belt of His waist. The wolf also shall dwell with the lamb, the leopard shall lie down with the young goat, the calf and the young lion and the fatling together; and A LITTLE CHILD SHALL LEAD THEM..."

Is this "little child" not the son of Adam whose representative is The Son of Man/Adam, i.e. Christ? Who else could this "little child" be? Surely this "little child" is no mere metaphor. Isaiah continues:

> "...The cow and the bear shall graze; their young ones shall lie down together; and the lion shall eat straw like the ox. The nursing CHILD shall play by the COBRA'S hole, and the weaned child shall put his hand in the VIPER'S den. They shall not hurt nor destroy in all My holy mountain, for the earth shall be full of the KNOWLEDGE of the Lord as the waters cover the sea," (Isaiah 11:1-9).

So here, in Isaiah 11:1-9, we have a picture of the restored Eden: the Tree of Life, carnivorous beings restored to their original design as herbivores, the infant son of Adam, alive and at peace, and all held in perfect harmony and felicity.

CHAPTER SEVEN

NEAR OBLIVION

How did all of these things remain forgotten for so long? There are many answers, but let us focus on only a few, and let us keep in mind that, strangely, in New Testament and Talmudic times, the death of a baby prior to the age of 30 days old was not considered (by the masses) anything over which to lament — in total contradiction to the Torah.

Jeremiah 8:8 criticizes the Scribes for having altered the Torah:

> "How can you say 'We are wise, for we have the Torah of the Lord,' when THE LYING PEN of the scribes has handled it falsely?"

It would be advantageous for the reader to ask, "Which part of the Torah was handled falsely by the Scribes since the *Bible* is telling me so?" *The Babylonian Talmud's* "Ketubot" openly distinguishes between the "teachings of the Torah" and the "teachings of the Scribes."

Let us turn to consider that when Herod slew the babies in his attempt to kill the Christ Child, it was Rachel who was "weeping for her children and refusing to be comforted because they are no more" (Matthew 2:18; Jeremiah 31:15); but Rachel, the wife of Israel, lived long before Christ's earthly days, and to understand this time-lapse, we must recall the circumstances between the time of Ezra and the earthly days of Christ.

By the time of Ezra, the Jews no longer read Hebrew. Knowledge of the Hebrew Scriptures was confined to a handful of elites, as is made plain in Nehemiah 8:8, for such is the reason that Ezra had to read and interpret Scripture for the people (note the Hebrew wordplay on "miscarriage" in Nehemiah 8:8). By the time of the return from Babylon, the knowledge of Hebrew had been erased from the majority of the Jewish people, and the situation was little different (though disastrously corrupt) during the days when Christ walked the earth. Again, neither the common Jews in the days of Ezra nor the common Jews during New Testament times spoke or read Hebrew, and the knowledge of Hebrew was confined to a small segment of the populace (see the *Babylonian Talmud's* "Yoma").

The Jews called the Torah the "Written Law." However, by the earthly days of Christ, the religious elites had been claiming, for some time, that God told Moses other laws that were not written down, and the collection of these laws was called "Oral Law." The difficulty in understanding the various arguments between Christ and the Pharisees is diminished greatly if one recognizes that though the "Law" is a continual discussion, the "Law" the Pharisees referred to was the supposed "Oral Law" and the "Law" that Christ referred to was the Torah, the "Written Law." The chief doctrine of the Pharisees (and of their offspring, the Rabbis of Judaism) was that the "Oral Law" was necessary to understand the "Written Law," and the Scribes usually sided with the Pharisees. The fallacious "Oral Law" was superimposed over the Torah by the Scribes, and the Torah became mistakenly thought of as "Judaism" despite the fact that there was no "Jewish" nation when the Torah was written. When the Torah was written, the only people on the earth who could be called "Jews" were those of the tribe of Judah, and Moses was of the tribe of Levi. To call the Torah "Judaism" would then disqualify the remaining tribes. The Torah was not a product of "Judaism" because "Judaism" did not exist when the Torah was written. For "... the Jews were entrusted with the oracles of God" (Romans 3:2) even though the Jews did not write the Torah. The Jews did invent the "Oral Law" that they called "Torah" or "Law" in mimicry of the Torah penned by Moses, and they mandated that this (oral) "Torah" was essential to follow in order to be in compliance with the Torah given through Moses.

The term "Oral Law" is, for practical purposes, synonymous with the idea of "Tradition" and can be thought of in the same sense as a philosophy, or a lens that interprets, or claims to interpret, Scripture; by this, I mean that the Tradition (*Mishnah*, *Gemara*, and thus, *Talmud*, etc.) is not so much evidence of Biblical history as it is evidence of a people-group who had forgotten and lost their own history — so they invented a "history" and deemed this hoax to be Scriptural; this invented "history" or "tradition" is the "Oral Law" that defines "Judaism." Basically, the "Oral Law" (at best) attempted to, or (at worst) pretended to supply the context for the Torah. However, since the "Oral Law" was not yet written (as we know it today) during the earthly days of Christ, the so-called "Oral Law" (that the Jews called "Torah") was subject to whatever elite spoke it; whatever subordinate heard it was subjected to the elite by the strength of a set of unwritten "laws" that pretended to originate from Sinai.

The origin of the "Oral Law" was a legend that sought to supply not only a history that the Jews had lost, but also a context that formed a world that the religious elites during the New Testament times desired to live within and control. When this legendary "Oral Law" became written, it resulted in the

Mishnah and eventuated into *Talmud*. The *Mishnah's* "Abot" distinguishes itself from the Torah of Moses when it states,

> "...he who exposes aspects of the Torah not in accord with the law... will have no share in the world to come."

If the Torah and the "law" of the Jews in the earthly days of Christ were one and the same, then the Pharisees themselves would not have distinguished between these two, as is plainly stated above. Basically, the Jewish elites during the earthly days of Christ claimed that pointing out contradictions in the law (that is, between their "Oral Law" and the Torah of God) mandated damnation. "The Law" of the Jews and the Law of God **were two different things** during the earthly days of Christ (as is true today), but they were both called "The Law" (as is also true today); it is for this reason that the accusations forwarded against Christ by the Pharisees **CANNOT** be found anywhere in the Torah, but the rules they wrangled over can be found in the *Talmud*, the Tradition. The Tradition (the "Oral Law") did not always seek to explain the Torah ("Written Law"), but it often contradicted the Torah; Christ pointed this out when He said,

> "...for the sake of your tradition, you make void the Word of God," (Matthew 15:6).

It must be remembered that there was no "Jewish" nation when the Torah was written. The "Jewish" nation began long after Moses (the Levite) penned the Torah. To say that there was a "Jewish" nation or a "Jewish" people in the days of Moses (beyond the tribe of Judah) would be like saying that there was a "Levite" nation in those days... for the people of Judah and the people of Levi were of the same Israelite people-group who had no geographical nation of their own. So, to claim that there was a "Jewish" nation in the time of

Moses would inherently contradict the claim that the Torah is "Judaism" since, by this mistake, the Torah would then have to be the product of a Levite nation and Levitism. However, when one reads a Jewish *Bible*, the term "Jew" is often used indiscriminately to discuss Hebrews and Israelites, and because of such a misnomer, people of the Church have been taught incorrectly since youth, even to the extent that some of us share in the guilt of having published so in a mistaken attempt to be in righteous compliance...

As far as physical descent is concerned, "Jews" are but a fraction of the Israelites of whom Moses was a familial member, and Israelites are but the physical descendents of Abraham the Hebrew. A "Hebrew" was never, nor is now, defined by nationality, for there was no "Hebrew" nation when Abraham was called a "Hebrew" (one who "passed over" into covenant with God). God's covenant with Abraham was specifically to the "Nations" which is the very same Hebrew word as "Gentiles." In English *Bibles*, the word "Gentiles" is employed in Galatians 3, but "Gentiles" and "nations" are the same Hebrew word. Furthermore:

Galatians 3:8-9: "And the Scripture, foreseeing that God would justify the *Gentiles* by faith, preached the gospel to Abraham beforehand, saying, 'In you all the *nations* shall be blessed.' So then those who are of faith are blessed with believing Abraham."

Genesis 12:3: "I will bless those who bless you, and I will curse him who curses you; and in you all the משפחת האדמה *families of the earth* shall be blessed."

Genesis 17:5:   "No longer will you be called Abram; your name will be Abraham, for I have made you a father of many גוים *nations*."

Genesis 18:18:   "And the Lord said, 'Shall I hide from Abraham what I am doing, since Abraham shall surely become a great and mighty nation, and all the גויי הארץ *nations of the earth* shall be blessed in him?'"

The word גוים means both "nations" and "gentiles," and one can read in an English *Bible* of the גוים *gentiles* and the גוים *nations* in the very same passage (Genesis 10:5) and understand that the same word is employed for both "gentiles" and "nations" before any "Jews" walked the earth. The blessing under discussion was first pronounced when there was no "Jewish" nation and prior to any Israelites being on the earth. Therefore, when there were no Jews, there were no Gentiles; after there were Jews, then there were Gentiles. Hence, the Apostle Paul (a Jew) openly quoted from the Torah (that was not Jewish) regarding the blessing to the "nations" and to the "families" of the earth that were not defined by or restricted to physical descent. Since Paul's Jewish adversaries had been teaching that the Torah was Jewish, despite the fact that it is not, we can see how the storm brewed and the fracture occurred. When there is a common belief that one can learn the Word of God without consulting the written Word of God, we can see how both "Jews" and "Christians" alike rely heavily on an oral tradition that exists quite independently from Scripture. Again, Abraham was not Jewish, Moses was not Jewish, and the Torah is not Jewish.

"Jews" and "Christians" have used the words "Jew," "Israelite," and "Hebrew" synonymously, when these words are certainly not synonyms. A "Hebrew," as the root of this word implies, is one who "passes over" into covenant with God, regardless of one's nationality. An "Israelite" and a "Jew" are those of a certain physical descent. In order to understand what a "Hebrew" is, one would have to understand what a threshold covenant is, and the specificities of the threshold covenant were not altogether understood by the doctors of the Oral Law since such a covenant's history had long been forgotten. Unfortunately, neither space nor time allows us to digress into the mechanics of the threshold covenant. For now, let it be understood that a person had to "pass over" a threshold spiritually, and a physical crossing often accompanied this spiritual decision as a sign, in order to be a "Hebrew" like Abraham. For instance, the title "Hebrew" comes from the root עבר to pass over; Abraham "passed over" the River *Fruitful* (*Euphrates*) because he believed God, and so God made Abraham "fruitful" (Genesis 17:6). We may therefore glean more of the importance of this teaching:

> "I am the true vine, and my Father is the gardener. He cuts off every branch in me that bears no fruit, while every branch that does BEAR FRUIT he prunes so that it will be even more FRUITFUL. You are already clean because of the word I have spoken to you. Remain in me, and I will remain in you. No branch can BEAR FRUIT by itself; it must remain in the vine. Neither can you BEAR FRUIT unless you remain in me. I am the vine; you are the branches. If a man remains in me and I in him, he will BEAR MUCH FRUIT; apart from me you can do nothing. If anyone does not remain in me, he is like a branch that is thrown away and withers; such branches are picked up, thrown into the fire and burned. If you remain in me and my words remain in you, ask whatever you wish, and it will be given you. This is to my Father's glory, that you BEAR MUCH FRUIT, showing yourselves to BE MY DISCIPLES," (John 15:1-8).

Someone's fruitful, new nature was evidence of their covenant with God. We can understand more of why Christ used a vine to craft this particular statement when we reflect on the fact that, during the time these words were spoken, the vine had been long understood as the tree that exhibited two births, thus the doctrine of being "born again." That is, Diodorus Siculus informs us that the ancients accounted the first "birth" of the vine to be when "the plant is set in the ground and begins to grow," and that "a second birth when it becomes laden with fruit and ripens its clusters," and this is why the pagans thought that the vine-god Dionysus was "born once from the earth and again from the vine," (*Library of History*, Diodorus; Book III.62). If one has a "belief" in Christ and yet bears no fruit beyond his own belief, such barrenness is evidence of the fact that such an individual has *not* been born again, and so we have the Book of *James*. To say the so-called "sinner's prayer" and to employ it little differently than a magic spell, then to continue with life as usual completely contradicts the significance of the vine and the threshold referred to above as such a weak declaration perverts the very idea of being "born again." However, modern Western society has forgotten what a "covenant" is, and it seems only to understand "contracts." Such a pitiful situation is a nearly insurmountable stumbling-block and has evinced itself in the ravaging plight of divorce that has resulted from "marriages" undertaken without any knowledge of covenants whatsoever.

The covenant between God and Abraham never involved "Jews" exclusively because "Jews" did not exist when the covenant was given. "Jews" are now a national group as well as a group linked by physical descent, and not all Jews are "Hebrews"; furthermore, if one were to pretend that Jews existed in the days of Abraham, then by this breach of reason and chronology, Abraham himself would have been a Gentile since he was a Chaldean. Some Jews are Hebrews, but not all Hebrews are Jews. One who follows God, that is, one who "passes over" into covenant with God is a "Hebrew," but one who is a "Jew" is not necessarily one who follows God. A "Jew" is one of a certain physical descent; a "Hebrew" is one of a certain belief. The claim that the Torah is "Jewish" is surely a logical fallacy and a mistake of chronology. "Christianity" did not come from "Judaism," and if "Christians" stopped letting outsiders define "Christianity," then they would grasp that one of the central arguments of the New Testament is that the belief now called "Christianity" is the return to the religion of Abraham that had been corrupted by the invention of Judaism. The Pharisees combined traces of the Torah with an oral philosophy and an invented tradition based on national identity and thereby formed the upstart faith called "Judaism" that did not exist when Moses penned the Torah. Since such has been confused for so long, we can begin to comprehend how it has been believed erroneously that God planted the forbidden tree and that the forbidden tree imparted wisdom and death simultaneously in direct contradiction to Scripture when it states that wisdom gives life (Ecclesiastes 7:11-12).

The legalities that the Pharisees accused Christ of breaking were not Biblical, though the Pharisees claimed that such legalities originated from Moses; Christ argued from the Torah, but the Pharisees argued from their "Oral Law," which served, basically, as national Jewish law under the pretense of Torah study — and the common man could no longer read the Torah in its original language during the earthly days of Christ. The Pharisees claimed that since Deuteronomy 18:15 stated that the people were to heed "The Prophet" (and they considered themselves to be this "Prophet" collectively), then the people were to heed them as group (*Babylonian Talmud:* "Yebamot"). "The Prophet" of Deuteronomy 18:15 was Christ, and the Pharisees had attempted to usurp His authority.

Since the word מָשַׁל can mean both *to rule* and *to riddle*, we can see how the "serpent" of Genesis 3 attempted to usurp the authoritative reign of the son of Man by asking a question (a riddle), and so Christ, The Son of Adam, referred to the Pharisees as "serpents" as well (Matthew 12:34). The reader will notice that many riddles were propounded on both sides of the various arguments preserved in the Gospels. Let us examine Deuteronomy 18:15-20:

> "The Lord your God will raise up for you a Prophet like me from your midst, from your brethren. Him you shall hear, according to all you desired of the Lord your God in Horeb in the day of the assembly, saying, 'Let me not hear again the voice of the Lord my God, nor let me see this great fire anymore, lest I die.' And the Lord said to me: 'What they have spoken is good. I will raise up for them a Prophet like you from among their brethren, and will put My words in His mouth, and He shall speak to them all that I command Him. And it shall be that whoever will not hear My words, which He speaks in My name, I will require it of him. But the prophet who presumes to speak a word in My name, which I have not commanded him to speak, or who speaks in the name of other gods, THAT PROPHET SHALL DIE.'"

According to the *Babylonian Talmud's* "Yebamot," the elites during the earthly days of Christ believed that they were the "Prophet" discussed above, and the fact that Christ opposed them mandated (in their eyes) that He be put to death. However, Peter understood that, truly, the "Prophet" of Deuteronomy 18:15 was Christ, and so he referred to this passage in Acts 3:21-23:

> "Repent therefore and be converted, that your sins

may be blotted out, so that times of refreshing may come from the presence of the Lord, and that He may send JESUS CHRIST, who was preached to you before, whom heaven must receive until the times of restoration of all things, which God has spoken by the mouth of all His holy prophets since the world began. For MOSES truly said to the fathers, 'The Lord your God will raise up for you a PROPHET like me from your brethren. Him you shall hear in all things, whatever He says to you. And it shall be that every soul who will not hear that Prophet shall be utterly destroyed from among the people.'"

After the Ascension, anyone who taught that Christ was indeed the "Prophet" of Deuteronomy 18:15 would have been perceived as one who directly attacked the social and religious order of the day by having exposed the Pharisees' misunderstanding and deceitfulness. Therefore, Stephen, having preached Christ, said:

"This is that MOSES who said to the children of Israel 'The Lord your God will raise up for you a PROPHET like me from your brethren. Him you shall hear.' This is he who was in the congregation in the wilderness with the Angel who spoke to him on Mount Sinai, and with our fathers, the one who received the living oracles to give to us, whom our fathers would not obey, but rejected. And in their hearts they turned back to Egypt, saying to Aaron, 'Make us gods to go before us; as for this Moses who brought us out of the land of Egypt, we do not know what has become of him,'" (Acts 7:37-40).

As recorded in the *Babylonian Talmud's* "Yebamot," the religious elites during the New Testament times (who thought that they were, collectively, the "Prophet") claimed that it was their privilege to alter the Torah (or the practice of it) since they said, "Everything is relative to the moment." That is, these elites (the Pharisees, the Jewish lawyers, the Scribes...) were not moral legalists according to Scripture. I repeat, the Jewish elites were not moral legalists! The Jewish elites during the earthly days of Christ were, instead, moral relativists; they felt free to make up their own laws apart from Scripture, but they mandated that subordinates strictly adhere to whatever alterations to the Torah the elites exacted at will (*Mishnah*: "Horayot" 1:1); thus, Christ said,

> "Woe to you also, lawyers! For you load men with burens hard to bear, AND YOU YOURSELVES DO NOT TOUCH THE BURDENS WITH ONE OF YOUR FINGERS [see *Mishnah*: "Horayot" 1:1]. Woe to you! For you build the TOMBS of the prophets, and your fathers killed them. In fact, you bear witness that you approve the deeds of your fathers; for they indeed killed them, and you build their TOMBS. Therefore the wisdom of God also said, 'I will send them prophets and apostles, and some of them they will kill and persecute,' that the blood of all the prophets which was shed from the foundation of the world may be required of this generation, from the blood of Abel to the blood of Zechariah who perished between the altar and the temple. Yes, I say to you, it shall be required of this generation. Woe to you lawyers! For YOU HAVE TAKEN AWAY THE KEY OF KNOWLEDGE. You did not enter in yourselves, and those who were entering in you hindered," (Luke 11:46-52).

Notice that Christ spoke of "tombs" in the passage above in light of His repeated accusations of hypocrisy against those to whom He directed this statement. A corpse buried in the soil, and innocent human blood that is shed upon the earth, causes the soil to be cursed and polluted. The word חָנֵף means *to defile* and *to profane* as a verb (Numbers 35:33; Isaiah 24:5, Jeremiah 3:1; 3:2; 3:9; 23:11, Psalm 106:38, Micah 4:11) and this word can also be used to indicate a *hypocrite* (Job 8:13; 13:16; 15:34; 17:8; 20:5; 27:8; 34:30; 36:13; Psalm 35:16, Proverbs 11:9, Isaiah 9:17; 10:6; 33:14). Therefore, it stands to reason why the very people whom Christ referred to as *hypocrites* were also accused by Him as being responsible for *innocent blood*. So, we see that the "brood of vipers" was a group of hypocritical shedders of innocent blood, and The Son of Adam identified them as such; that is, we can see the serpent and the son of Adam in Eden by observing the serpents and The Son of Adam in Jerusalem. As the son of Adam died innocently on account of others' misconduct and misunderstanding by way of a tree, so we can see how The Son of Man died innocently on account of others' misconduct and misunderstanding by way of a tree.

In the *Babylonian Talmud's* "Yebamot," the elites claimed that they had the right to violate the Torah on the grounds that they were given such authority from on high because they claimed that Deuteronomy 18:15 allowed them to command others to break the Torah, and that such a breach of God's Word was righteous, so long as it was commanded by them. So, Deuteronomy 18:15 was the Written Law, but the Pharisees' basic claim was that such a law could not be interpreted without them and their "Oral Law" which they pretended originated with Moses, even though it often contradicted what Moses wrote (as is even admitted by them). So long as believers did not (or could not) actually read the Torah in Hebrew, the Pharisees appeared to be strict legalists, which was, of course, not true since they were the exact opposite. Is this not true of the "serpent" also? Along with the relativists' self-proclaimed right to alter the Torah, the same Talmudic portion under discussion cites a deliberately false trial that the Pharisees themselves exacted (against the regulations of the Torah), where they killed a man so as to "establish a fence around the Torah." That is, it was actually the contradictory doctrine of the Oral Law that if people do not even get close to breaking the Torah because of extra-Biblical laws (even if such extra-Biblical laws defy the *Bible* in the end), a righteous religious jurisdiction has occurred... and such was the "reasoning" behind the false trial of Christ... such is the "reasoning" why "Tradition" has mandated beliefs concerning talking snakes, magic fruit, and other forms of nonsense that birth contradiction after contradiction.

Webster's II New College Dictionary defines "legalism" as "the strict, literal adherence to the law." Since Books like Romans and Galatians thoroughly explain that we are on the pre-circumcised Abraham-plan (so to speak), we are fulfilling the covenant that preceded Sinai through Christ's fulfillment of all 613 laws of the Torah according to the prophecy in Eden. Since many who identify themselves with the Church do not regularly read the Torah, they have accidentally assumed that the doctrine of the Pharisees came from the Torah (which was the FALSE CLAIM of the Pharisees themselves) despite Christ's statement negating such an assumption in Matthew 15:6; accordingly, a false definition of "legalism" became associated with the Pharisees, and this "legalism" became repugnant to many who identify themselves with the Church; a similar situation occurred in Eden, and the bride has continued to consume others out of defiance and in a departure from the Word of God. Despite the misunderstanding, it must be understood that the Pharisees were moral relativists, not Scriptural legalists, for Christ specifically said,

"...not one of you keeps the Torah," (John 7:19).

Question: Why has it been taught to us from our youth
             that the Pharisees were Scriptural legalists
             when Christ Himself says plainly that they were
             not?

Answer: Oral Tradition has been preferred to the written
             Word of God.

Again, even if one never read the Torah, but only read the
Gospels, how could one who believes the words of Christ
claim that the Pharisees were somehow legalists when Christ
Himself said that they did not keep the Torah?

In the introduction to brilliant English translation of the
Mishnah (the "Oral Law") accomplished by Jacob Neusner,
Neusner wrote,

> "Nor should we fail to notice, even at the outset, that
> while the *Mishnah* clearly addresses Israel, the Jewish
> people, it is remarkably indifferent to the Hebrew
> Scriptures," (p. xiii).

In reaction to the *Mishnah's* seemingly strange design,
Neusner went on to ask and to state,

> "Who would want to have made such a thing? Who
> would now want to refer to it? The answer to those
> questions is deceptively straightforward: the *Mishnah*
> is important because it is a principal component in the
> cannon of Judaism," (p. xiv).

Once again, we observe a distinct difference between
"Judaism" and the "Old Testament." According to followers
of "Judaism," the Old Testament is only one of the sacred
texts of Judaism; strangely enough, Judaism claims that

the Hebrew Scriptures can be broken righteously. What is called "Judaism" is not merely Old Testament study, for there are volumes upon volumes that Judaism falsely considers to be "Holy Scripture." Furthermore, Neusner's introduction admits that the "sages" who composed the *Mishnah* often dealt with subjects of which they

> "...had no material access or practical knowledge at the time of their work," (p. xvi).

The "Oral Law," being oral, was whatever the elites said it was, and such assertions were exacted on the strength that it was Moses, and not these elites, who taught contradictory doctrines. In fact, the "Oral Law" goes so far as to blame God for the Israelites' golden calf idolatry (*Babylonian Talmud:* "Berakhot"). The *Talmud* is infamous for having invented fictitious conversations between God and Moses that are not recorded in Scripture. Having established a brief historical overview, let us turn to the account of Joseph, in the Book of Genesis.

The Israelites would not have come to Egypt had it not been for Joseph's maneuvering with Benjamin. During the time of Joseph, Benjamin was the key to the Israelites' perpetuity (Genesis 44:12-33). Jacob (Israel) labored specifically for Rachel, and he loved her especially, even to the point that he placed her geographically farthest away from the potential hazard of Genesis 33:2. In other words, Jacob provided special protection for his greatest romantic, human love, his wife Rachel; Jacob guarded Rachel with particular caution. Then, the Torah tells us that,

> "...they journeyed from Bethel. And when there was but a little distance to go to Ephrath, Rachel labored in childbirth, and SHE HAD HARD LABOR. Now it came to

pass, when she was in HARD LABOR, that the midwife said to her, 'Do not fear; you will have this son also.' And so it was, as her soul was departing (for she died), that she called his name Ben-Oni; but his father called him Benjamin. So Rachel died and was buried on the way to Ephrath (that is, BETHLEHEM)," (Genesis 35:16-19).

However, by the time of the fallacious invention of the Oral Law, the precedence of life was reversed against the Written Torah. That is, just before Jesus' earthly days, it had become a *Jewish* (Oral) law — in opposition to the *Hebrew* (Written) Law — that when a woman endured "hard labor," the religious elites permitted abortion:

"The woman who is in HARD LABOR — they chop up the child in her womb and they remove it limb by limb, because her life takes precedence over his life," (*Mishnah*: "Ohalot" 7:6).

However, this *Jewish* law stated above had nothing to do with the *Hebrew* Scriptures, which helps further explain the major contention between Christ and the morally relative elites of His earthly days. The Hebrew Torah illustrated that Benjamin's life took precedence over Rachel's life, but the doctors of the Jewish Oral Law claimed that the mother's life took precedence over the child's life. The *Bible* is quite clear that the good works, alone, of humans do not save humans from damnation; yet, humans are still required to perform good works as a display of faith, thus the Book of James and the faith of Abraham.

It has been erroneously asserted that the Jewish elites during the earthly days of Christ were "legalists" and that they were errant *because* they followed God's Law strictly, when they did not follow God's Torah strictly. However, such a faulty claim cannot hold up when we read the Torah's 613 laws and find that not a single accusation given by the Pharisees and Sadducees can be found in the Torah! — not one! The religious elites during the earthly days of Christ were hardly legalists with respect to Biblical Law, for they deliberately abrogated the Torah on a consistent basis in order to establish their own laws (the "Oral Law"); for the *Babylonian Talmud's* "Yebamot" states,

"Everything is relative to the moment,"

which is precisely why Christ was given a phony trial, and the Pharisees' blatant statement that "Everything is relative to the moment" immediately precedes their discussion of how they gave a man a false trial and killed him because, "the times required it"; the *Babylonian Talmud's* "Sanhedrin" repeats the same philosophy and ruling. "Legalism," with respect to the Torah, did not exist amongst the religious elites whom Christ criticized. "Legalism" simply means "the strict, literal adherence to the law." Since Christ was the only One ever to fulfill all 613 commandments of the Torah, He was, by strict definition, the most "legalistic" Person ever to live (for Christ followed the Law, the Torah, out of a pure, loving heart, not out of mere obligation) [note 6, p. 171]. Had the Pharisees and Sadducees actually been legalists with respect to the Torah, then they would have drawn closer to fulfilling the Torah themselves, and they would have unanimously recognized that Christ fulfilled all 613 regulations of the Torah precisely — out of love (even with respect to the 365 negative commandments). For instance, it is a Torah law to love one's neighbor as oneself (Leviticus 19:18), but the Pharisees and Sadducees did not, and the very next passage of the Torah states, "...You shall not sow your field with mixed seed..." (Leviticus 19:19), which is the very thing that was done to produce the forbidden tree in Eden. The *Mishnah* (and the subsequent *Talmuds*), i.e. the preserved, and sometimes augmented, record of the Jewish law of Jesus' earthly days, blatantly defied the Torah; since Jesus exposed this fact to the masses, the religious elites of the day sought to kill Him based on their invented religious authority to assert that, "Everything is relative to the moment." Basically, the *Talmud* is to the *Bible* what U.S. Law is to the *Bible* ; U.S. law does not align seamlessly with Scripture, and, at many points, U.S. law deliberately defies Scripture.

The Pharisees were,

> "an essentially LAY GROUP formed from one of the branches of the Hasidim of the Maccabaean age," (*The Complete Dead Sea Scrolls*, Vermes; p. 53). "After the ephemeral rule of the successor to Herod the Great, Herod Archelaus (4 BCE-6 CE), who was deposed by Augustus for his misgovernment of Jews and Samaritans alike, Galilee continued in semi-autonomy under the Herodian princes Antipas (4 BCE- 39 CE) and Agrippa (39-41 CE), but Judaea was placed under the direct administration of Roman authority. In 6 CE, Coponius, the first Roman prefect of Judaea, arrived to take up his duties there. This prefectorial regime, whose most notorious representative was Pontius Pilate (26-36 CE), lasted for thirty-five years until 41, when the emperor Claudius appointed Agrippa I as king. He died, however, three years later, and in 44 CE the government of the province once more reverted to Roman officials, this time with the title of procurator. Their corrupt and unwise handling of Jewish affairs was one of the chief causes of the war of 66 which led to the destruction of Jerusalem in 70 CE, and to the subsequent decline of the Sadducees, the extinction of the Zealots in Masada in 74, the

disappearance of the Essenes, and the survival and **uncontested domination of the Pharisees and their rabbinic successors**," (*The Complete Dead Sea Scrolls*, Vermes; p. 53). (The highlighting is of Joshua Collins and not of the original author).

Rabbinic Judaism finds its roots in the order of the Pharisees. As such, terms like "Jew," "Israelite," and "Hebrew" have become (falsely) interchangeable, even though they are not synonymous.

To say that Abraham was "Jewish" is like saying that Christopher Columbus' great-grandfather was "American." That עבר *Eber* (Genesis 10:24), the great grandson of Shem, was an ancestor of Abraham, and that the name *Eber* shares the same root as the title "Hebrew" does not necessitate that a mere patronymic that preceded the covenant given to Abraham is the sole basis for the word "Hebrew." Specifically, Abraham was one who עבר *passed over* into covenant with God before his grandson was renamed "Israel." Abraham "passed over" the River *Fruitful* (*Euphrates*) because he believed God, and so God made Abraham "fruitful" (Genesis 17:6). Abraham did something because of his belief; he did not believe and do nothing. "Jews," as they are called, did not come into existence until after the "Israelites." Hebrews 11:9 tells us that Abraham lived in tents with Isaac and Jacob (Israel), as the Torah points out that Abraham was 100 years old when Isaac was born (Genesis 21:5) and that he lived to be 175 years old (Genesis 25:6), and since Isaac was 60 years old at the births of Esau and Jacob (Genesis 25:26), then these grandchildren of Abraham were only 15 years old when Abraham died. Since Judah was the child of Jacob (Israel), after Jacob fled from Esau, since the descendants of Judah came after Abraham was dead, and since there was no land of Judah in Abraham's day, it is quite contrary to state that Abraham was a Jew when "Jews" came from the physical line of Abraham, as did the Ishmaelites. Accordingly, when we take into account that the Jewish law was often opposed to the Hebrew Torah, that Abraham was not a "Jew" or an "Israelite" (for Jacob, i.e. Israel, was his descendant), and when we take into account that Jacob was the first "Israelite" (so to speak), then we will notice that the "Jewish" law during the earthly days of Christ was not original, for we can observe that Rachel died at childbirth, despite the *Mishnah*'s provision for abortion aimed at preferring a mother's life... a provision that could have claimed the life of Benjamin in order to spare the life of Rachel. Such infanticide/child-sacrifice (euphemistically called "abortion") was, in more places than one within Scripture, wholeheartedly repugnant to God and to the patriarchs (Deuteronomy 12:31; 18:10); but since child sacrifice had become rampant in Abraham's day, since child sacrifice was thought to be the ultimate sacrifice to a deity, and since there was no written Torah in the days of Abraham, Abraham was tested concerning what the cultures of his day perversely assumed was the greatest offering. Since Abraham was willing to exact such a sacrifice, his faith was proven and the horrid act was averted. In no way could God have desired or condoned the sacrifice of any child, for God stated, "...to burn their sons and their daughters in the fire, which I did not command, nor did it come into My heart" (Jeremiah 7:31); this may form at least part of the reason why Abraham explicitly stated that both he *and his son* would return *after* God told Abraham to sacrifice Isaac (Genesis 22:5) and why Isaac's return with his father Abraham (as Abraham himself prophesied) was considered a type of resurrection (Hebrews 11:19).

In the instance of "hard labor"— so called (since all such labor is "hard") — **it was the child who took precedence over the mother according to the Torah,** as such a point is more than obvious regarding the specific mother of Joseph and Benjamin, Jacob's love for Rachel, his protection of her, and her death... for it was her son, Benjamin, who was the critical person (Genesis 42: 20) who bound Joseph and his betraying brothers back together in order to set the Egyptian stage of Exodus. In complete contradiction to the Scriptural principle of life stated above, the *Mishnah* states that, "The woman who is in hard labor — they chop up the child in her womb and they remove it limb by limb, because her life takes precedence over his life," (Mishnah: "Ohalot" 7:6). Thus, we see that Rachel, who gave her life for her son, was buried by Bethlehem, and Herod slaughtered the infants of and around Bethlehem (Matthew 2:16); we can then understand why Matthew 2:18 quotes Jeremiah 31:15:

> "A voice was heard in Ramah, wailing and loud lamentation, RACHEL weeping for her children..."

for it was through Jeremiah that it was written,

> "Before I formed you in the womb, I knew you..." (Jeremiah 1:5).

The idea expressed above relates that Rachel died for her child and was buried in the very place that, in the earthly days of Christ, children were slain for the sake of an adult. Rachel's example of love was inverted by the lawyers during the earthly days of Christ. It is therefore evident, through Rachel, that, even though she was the most beloved woman of Jacob (Israel), her child's life took precedence over her own (in the days of the patriarchs), but by the earthly days of Christ, the exact opposite was the "Oral Law," i.e. the national Jewish laws that were often in direct opposition to the Hebrew Torah and the very laws that served as the basis for the contention between Christ and the religious elites of the day.

Christ never broke an ordinance of the Torah; when it was written that Christ broke the Sabbath in John 5:18, the "Sabbath" under discussion was not the Sabbath of the Torah, but rather the "Sabbath" that can be found in the *Talmud's* volume called "Shabbat," which is quite distinct from the Torah's Sabbath. Christ broke no Torah Law, but He did certainly break the Oral Laws that inflated and defied the Torah — His Torah. "Love does no harm to its neighbor. Therefore love is the fulfillment of the Torah," (Romans 13:10); accordingly, it is not out of "love" that one take the life of a child; rather,

> "Greater love has no one than this, than to lay down one's life for his friends" (John 5:13),

as Rachel laid her life down for her child! Since Rachel gave her life for Benjamin, it was Rachel, though long dead, who was described as "weeping" when children were killed for the sake of Herod in Matthew 2, for the children were killed near the place where Rachel was buried (Genesis 35:19). "Loving" God means strictly following His Word literally (I John 2:3), so we cannot purposely defy God's Word as an act of "love" towards Him. Before the Torah (the Written Law) was given, it was written that Abraham followed God's laws (Genesis 26:5) because Abraham believed in, and therefore followed God (James 2:23-24). How can one follow God if one does not carry out His Word? — ask a "Christian" who gives multiple arguments as to why he does not have to read Scripture regularly.

Even though the "Oral Law" displays an obvious variance with the Torah, it is, by far, the most descriptive history of the ancient Jews during the earthly days of Christ, even if such history must be gleaned from the evidence that those who wrote down the Oral Law had indeed forgotten their own history. Knowing that everything is written in reaction to something, it is evident that the discovery of facts must sometimes be accomplished by observing the reactions to those facts. Such is the case with the term "fruit of the tree." It is easy to think of the "fruit" under discussion as only that — "fruit." However, "Fruit of the Tree" was the name of wine unmixed with water (*Commentary on the New Testament from the Talmud and Hebraica*, Lightfoot; Vol. 2, p. 351). Many ancients mandated that wine was to be mixed with water in order to be deemed drinkable. Wine mixed with water was called "fruit of the vine" by the Hebrews, Israelites, and Jews, while the portion that was unmixed with water was called "fruit of the tree." Without water, the "fruit of the tree" was deemed undrinkable.

The *Bible* is the Word of God; the *Bible* is a perfect story because God is a perfect God... the only God. The *Bible* is a riddle, and God is the Ruler... the Riddler:

> "It is the glory of God to conceal a matter, but the glory of kings is to search out a matter," (Proverbs 25:2).

God created life. God created seed. God created the womb. God created light. All that is antithetical to God is a manipulation orchestrated by the Enemy. God created the Tree of Life. Satan manipulated God's creation, and, at the allowance of man (who did not rule over the Enemy), Satan planted death into the "midst" of "Eden" and into the midst of Eve's womb. The *Mishnah*'s "Nidda" states,

> "Women as regards [the blood of] virginity are like vines."

The *Mishnah*'s "Ohalot" discusses the gathering of grapes near graves. The word אשכל *grape-cluster* comes from the root *to suffer abortion, to bereave of children, to miscarry,* which helps explain the significance of Satan's false vine-tree, i.e. the Tree of the Knowledge of Good and Evil in the middle of Eden, the womb:

> "Now a river went out of Eden to water the garden, and from there it parted and became four riverheads. The name of the first is פישון *Diffusion of Waters*; it is the one which skirts the whole land of חוילה *Bringing Forth, especially of a pregnant woman*, where there is gold. And the gold of that land is good. Bdellium and the onyx stone are there. The name of the second river is גיחון *Belly, as the Source of the Fetus*; it is the one which goes around the whole land of כוש *The Womb* * [note 1, p. 167]. The name of the third river is חדקל *Light, Swift*; it is the one which goes toward the east of אשור *Lifted Up, Exalted*. The fourth river is the פרת *Fruitful*," (Genesis 2:10-14).

Since Scripture has not been understood as a riddle, people stopped looking for the answer to the riddle — which is the very word (or words) that cannot be stated within the riddle itself. The answer to the riddle of Genesis 1-3 is "paradise," which is precisely what Christ uttered on the tree of death (Luke 23:43) since the pregnancy of the paradise in Eden had been thwarted on account of a tree of death; for one may notice that "...in the place where He was crucified there was a GARDEN..." (John 19:41), and because of the tomb in it, it could not be rightfully called a "paradise," as was the case in Eden also.

Because the definition of a "paradise" has seldom been sought out, the arrogant claim that Genesis 1 and Genesis 2 exhibit corruption wrought by a primitive editor who was too stupid to notice that the first couple of pages in the Book were contradictory has dominated "Biblical" discussion. Accordingly, readers began to overlook the bold fact that

Genesis 2:4 states that the entirety of Creation took place within a "day" by claiming various positions based on the assumption of others' deficiencies in light of the Jewish vowel-points that were superimposed over the Hebrew Scriptures. Since the answer to the riddle of Eden is "paradise," we can comprehend how the answer to Fall is Paradise... how the answer to our errors and the banishment into death is God's forgiveness and the reconciliation unto life.

Since it has been forgotten that God, being perfectly just, articulated judgment against Adam prior to the creation of woman, it has been assumed that the woman was the first sinner, when, in truth, Adam did not "guard." Since "Christians" have not "guarded" against (and subsequently warred against) the seduction of shining screens, now every form of blasphemy and every manner of perversion dealing with fertility and unity is found on basic "family" programming continually and with increasing fervor. Such wretchedness is gobbled greedily by "brethren" who openly pray against the very things they fund on a monthly basis to the destruction of their own children. It is a baffling sight to watch one who spends dozens of hours per week yielding his own will and heart to a talking light-bulb openly mock those who once worshipped stars, when the very celebrities who own his mind he himself calls "stars." When study is shunned because feeling is preferred, then the employment of words like "Christian" and "love" take on whatever meaning the supplier desires in the guise of what is commonly (and erroneously) referred to as "Christianity," which then seems to prove the opposition's case that facts have little place in organized "Christianity." If indeed facts have little place in organized "Christianity," it is only because the *Bible* has little place in organized "Christianity"... which has produced the near oblivion under discussion. How was the Fall in Eden any different than the fall today? — only in that the humans actually knew that they had fallen in Eden.

How darkly amazing it is to consider that the word "serpent" in the Eden Narrative comes from the root נחש *to shine,* for it was this shining one's tactic to occupy human minds more so than the Word of God.

CONCLUSION

We have understood that God did not plant the forbidden tree. Now, let us consider seedless ("sterile," "barren") fruit along with the fact that "seed" was not mentioned among the food that was given to animals; if we connect this consideration of animal food to sterility, barrenness, and death, perhaps it will prove easier to decipher the words,

> "I said in my heart, "Concerning the condition of the sons of men, God tests them, that they may see that they themselves are like animals," (Ecclesiastes 3:18).

That is, strictly speaking, humanity was required to eat seed-bearing products, but animals were not:

> "And God said, 'See, I have given you every herb that yields seed which is on the face of all the earth, and every tree whose fruit yields seed; to you it shall be for food. Also, to every beast of the earth, to every bird of the air, and to everything that creeps on the earth, in which there is life, I have given EVERY GREEN HERB FOR FOOD'; and it was so," (Genesis 1:29-30).

There was no mention of seed with regard to the diet of the animals, which explains part of the reason why the Enemy is compared to a "serpent," though the word we render "serpent" is also used as a proper noun, i.e. a title, a personal name, in Scripture (I Samuel 11:1, for example). Therefore, it would be consistent for someone regarded as an animal to suggest consuming something seedless, barren, and sterile. At the same time, encapsulating the characters of people with animal descriptions was more than common, even amongst the heathen nations, during the times of the composition of Scripture; such was even true in visual art history as well. Accordingly, we may understand why the early Church, as a whole, did not believe in fairy-tales regarding talking snakes; Clement of Alexandria wrote in his *Exhortation to the Greeks*,

> "But far different is my minstrel, for He has come to bring to a speedy end the bitter slavery of the daemons that lord it over us; and by leading us back to the mild and kindly yoke of piety He calls once again to heaven those who have been cast down to earth. He at least is the only one who ever tamed the most intractable of all wild beasts — man: for he tamed birds, that is, flighty men; REPTILES, THAT IS, CRAFTY MEN; lions, that is, passionate men; swine, that is, pleasure-loving men; wolves, that is rapacious men. Men without understanding are stocks and stones; indeed a man steeped in ignorance is even more senseless than stones. As our witness let the prophetic voice, which shares in the song of truth, come forward, speaking words of pity for those who waste away their lives in ignorance and folly,— 'for God is able of these stones to raise up children unto Abraham [Matthew 3:9],'"

and again,

> "This was not the first time that He pitied us for our error. He did that from heaven from the beginning. But now by His appearing He has rescued us, when we were on the point of perishing. For the WICKED, CRAWLING WILD BEAST makes slaves of men by his magical arts, and torments them even until now,

exacting vengeance, as it seems to me, after the manner of barbarians, who are said to bind their captives to corpses until both rot together. Certain it is that wherever this wicked TYRANT AND SERPENT succeeds in making men his own FROM THEIR BIRTH, he rivets them to stocks, stones, statues and suchlike idols, by the miserable chain of daemon-worship; then he takes and buries them alive, AS THE SAYING GOES, until they also, men and idols together, suffer corruption. On this account (for it is one and the same deceiver who in the beginning carried off Eve to death, and now does the like to the rest of mankind) our rescuer and helper is one also, namely, the Lord, who from the beginning revealed Himself through prophesy, but now invites us plainly to salvation," (Clement of Alexandria, born roughly 150 A.D.).

Notice how Isaiah 14:12-16 refers to the "serpent" of Genesis 3 as a "man":

"How you are fallen from heaven, O Lucifer, son of the morning! How you are cut down to the ground, you who weakened the nations! For you have said in your heart: 'I will ascend into heaven, I will exalt my throne above the stars of God; I will also sit on the mount of the congregation the farthest sides of the north; I will ascend above the heights of the clouds, I will be like the Most High.' Yet you shall be brought down to Sheol, to the lowest depths of the Pit. Those who see you will gaze at you, and consider you, saying: 'Is this THE MAN who made the earth tremble, who shook kingdoms?'"

The angels are also called "men" (Luke 24:4). Antithetically, consider the religious elites of the Gospel times where it is written against them,

"...BROOD OF VIPERS! Who warned you to flee from the wrath to come? Therefore bear fruits worthy of repentance, and do not think to say to yourselves, 'We have Abraham as our father.' For I say to you that God is able to raise up children to Abraham from these stones. And even now the axe is laid to the root of the trees. Therefore every tree which does not bear good fruit is cut down and thrown into the fire," (Matthew 3:7-10).

Children are as impressionable as human "stones"; stones are the foundation of families, hence the idea of mental inferiority combined with children by the figure of a "stone"... which is exactly why we are commanded,

"Brothers and sisters, do not be children in your thinking. In regard to evil be infants, but in your thinking be adults," (I Corinthians 14:20).

We are instead to be as innocent as children, not as naive as children (Matthew 18:13; I Corinthians 14:20). In the book of Matthew alone, no one has any difficulty understanding that people are called "vipers" (3:7), "wolves" (7:15), "sheep" (10:6), and "goats" (25:33), and yet it is mandated by many, under supposed penalty of hell-fire, that reptiles spoke in antiquity.

The Hebrew Scriptures were, originally, written without vowels; to think of this in English, let us consider these consonants: "hsrd." We may vowelize these consonants to mean, "**He is rude**," "**He is red**," "**his road**," "**his ride**," "**his rod**," "**his raid**," etc. Which one is correct? Context is the key. The process of deduction that excludes induction altogether, and the choice of merely *this or that* as opposed to *this and that* is quite foreign to the Scriptures and can be attributed chiefly to a Western mindset that became almost uniformly super-imposed over an Eastern Book — the *Holy Bible*. The mad attempt to divorce the Old Testament from the New Testament has led to countless competing doctrines that many secular people truthfully accuse as fantastic, magical, and impossible. The New Testament simply cannot be understood at all without the Torah and the remainder of the Old Testament. Who could possibly comprehend any document by beginning with its latter quarter with a predetermined mindset to neglect its beginning, its premise, and its thesis?

The entirety of the *Bible* revolves around the first three chapters and the problem of sin, for after the conclusion of what we call Genesis "Chapter Three," the same story repeats until Revelation. The first three chapters of Scripture, in their sharp specificity, only make perfect sense in Hebrew, and the inspired writers of the New Testament must have known this. However, since Biblical Hebrew was already a dead language by the earthly days of Christ, it is historically evident and Scripturally proven (I Corinthians 2:1-14) that the Jewish elites during the times of Christ's earthly days did not know about the son of Adam; let us examine this point.

> "Then He said, 'Hear now MY WORDS: If there is a prophet among you, I, the Lord, make Myself known to him IN A VISION; I speak to him IN A DREAM. Not so with My servant Moses; he is faithful in all My house. I speak with him face to face, even plainly, and not IN DARK SAYINGS [בחידות *in riddles*]; and he sees the form of the Lord..."

Unless you are Moses resurrected, you can expect to be required to solve the "dark sayings" of God. Knowing that, linguistically, the mastery of riddles indicates mastery over people, we may notice that the so-called "serpent" of Genesis 3 did not tell humanity to do anything; he merely asked a question... that is, he propounded a riddle, and having mastery over the riddle, he gained mastery over the people.

The Torah refers to "poets" as "riddlers" in Numbers 21:27. Even in the heathen and secular world, the concealment of knowledge by riddle-telling was an understood principle; it would be helpful to notice that Aeschylus' play *The Suppliant Maidens* borrows much from Genesis 3. "...Moses was learned in all the wisdom of the Egyptians, and was mighty in words and deeds..." (Acts 7:22). The ancients who were taught Egyptian physiology were not taught the reasons of things, but were rather students of the highly-cultivated art of concealing knowledge beneath the surface of what at first seems to be a fantastic tale that stands particularly veiled from the commoner who lacked devotion in his/her study [note 7, p. 173]. In other words, and in our context, it was once expected that those who did not deliberately seek the answers to riddles would only be left with stories that seemed impossible, and under this supposition was Scripture written, for such a lack of loving devotion caused one to prove oneself profane... hence, II Corinthians 3:12-4:4:

> "Therefore, since we have such hope, we use great boldness of speech — unlike Moses, who put a veil over his face so that the children of Israel could not look steadily at the end of what was passing away. But their minds were blinded. For until this day the same veil remains unlifted in the reading of the Old Testament, because the veil is taken away in Christ. But even to this day, when Moses is read, a veil lies on their heart. Nevertheless when one turns to the Lord, the veil is taken away. Now the Lord is the Spirit; and where the Spirit of the Lord is, there is liberty. But we all, with unveiled face, beholding as in a mirror the glory of the Lord, are being transformed into the same image from glory to glory, just as by the Spirit of the Lord. Therefore, since we have this ministry, as we have received mercy, we do not lose heart. But we have

renounced the hidden things of shame, not walking in craftiness nor handling the word of God deceitfully, but by manifestation of the truth commending ourselves to every man's conscience in the sight of God. But even if our gospel is veiled, IT IS VEILED TO THOSE WHO ARE PERISHING, whose minds the god of this age has blinded, who do not believe, lest the light of the gospel of the glory of Christ, who is the image of God, should shine on them."

The word מָשַׁל means both *to rule* and *to riddle*; therefore, we may understand why Christ said, "To you it has been given to know the mystery [*to riddle*] of the kingdom [*to rule*] of God; but to those who are outside, all things come in parables [*riddles*], so that, 'Seeing they may see and not perceive, and hearing they may hear and not understand; lest they should turn, and their sins be forgiven them [Isaiah 6:9-10],'" (Mark 4:10-12). In fact, the Hebrew word דרשׁ *to seek* also means *to study* and *to tread*. Similarly, we can understand why Plato borrowed so heavily and deliberately from Genesis 1-3 when he composed his famous Atlantis narrative in his books *Timaeus* and *Critias*. There are specific reasons why the Book of Proverbs refers to the sayings of Amen-em-ope, why Titus 1:12 quotes Callimachus, why I Corinthians 15:33 quotes Menander, why Acts 17:28 quotes Aratus, etc.

I do not mean to assert that Scripture somehow copies the pattern of secular works. Scripture was not written to borrow from other religions and philosophies, but the religions and philosophies that existed in the days of the people to whom the various Books of Scripture were delivered served as historical back-drops and cultural contexts that engaged people, despite their misperceptions of the Divine, yet within their own respective cultures, in order to illustrate the uniformity of truth despite one's own geographical origin and initial cultural limitations. There must be some agreed-upon context under which all communication exists, otherwise a lack of communication is produced. What communication exists that is not reactionary? Of course, it was by such quotation and reference (as displayed above) that a foundational context was laid for the benefit of outsiders in order for those outsiders to become followers of the True and Only God. For those who did not "study" and "tread" in order to "seek" out the answer to a riddle, all that was left for them were seemingly imaginative stories about talking snakes, magic fruit, and the like. It is therefore evident that it is a detrimental practice to invent and to superimpose a foreign context onto a piece of written communication that was not written in reaction to such a context.

I had a friend from Kenya live with me for a couple of weeks. My next-door neighbor fed his dog steak. The dog reacted so positively that my next-door neighbor told my Kenyan friend that his dog "died and went to heaven"; my Kenyan friend recoiled in disgusted horror and asked, "Why did you kill your dog?" because he did not have such an expression in his native language, and he did not understand the expression in English; innocently, he took my next-door neighbor's words at face-value and thus misunderstood my neighbor's intended message. Both my Kenyan friend and my neighbor were about the same age. Ponder how much more difficult communication can become for people who are not only separated by entire oceans, cultures, and languages, but more so by thousands of years.

Since we have understood that a man's nakedness (specifically, a father's nakedness) can refer to his *wife's flesh*, then we can also understand how a man and his bride become "one flesh" (Genesis 2:24). Adam's side was opened for the sake of his bride (Genesis 2:21), just as Christ's side was opened for the sake of His bride (John 19:34). Consider the riddle of Ephesians 5:25-33:

> "Husbands, love your WIVES, just as Christ also loved the CHURCH and gave Himself for her, that He might sanctify and cleanse her with the washing of water by the word, that He might present her to Himself a glorious church, not having spot or wrinkle or any such thing, but that she should be holy and without blemish. So husbands ought to love THEIR OWN WIVES as THEIR OWN BODIES; he who loves HIS WIFE loves HIMSELF. For no one ever hated HIS OWN FLESH, but nourishes and cherishes it, just as the Lord does the church. For we are members of His BODY, of His FLESH and of His BONES [Genesis 2:23]. 'For this reason a man shall leave his father and mother and be joined to his wife, and the two shall become ONE FLESH.' This is a great mystery, BUT I SPEAK CONCERNING CHRIST AND THE CHURCH. Nevertheless let each one of you in particular so love his own WIFE AS HIMSELF, and let the wife see that she respects her husband.

The very fact that Biblical Hebrew was first written without vowels indicates how fertile soil was spread for the cultivation of the art of the enigma. With the art of the enigma comes the art of dominion; hence, the Book we commonly call "Proverbs" is the Hebrew מִשְׁלֵי, which can indicate *dominion* (that is, how to *rule*) and *riddles* (that is, *proverbs, parables, similitudes, dark sayings*, etc.):

> "The proverbs of Solomon the son of David, king of Israel: to know wisdom and instruction, to perceive the words of understanding, to receive the instruction of wisdom, justice, judgment, and equity; to give prudence to the simple, to the young man knowledge and discretion — a wise man will hear and increase learning, and a man of understanding will attain wise

counsel, to understand A PROVERB AND AN ENIGMA, the words of THE WISE AND THEIR RIDDLES," (Proverbs 1:1-6).

Recall how the great Fall of Man narrative in Genesis 3 revolves around "wisdom" and that "wisdom" and "abortion" are both indicated by the letters שכל (distinguishing between the sibilants). Recall how people have consistently blamed God for killing the Egyptian babies at the first Passover, when He did not. We have a clue provided in Revelation 11:8: "And their dead bodies will lie in the street of the great city which SPIRITUALLY IS CALLED SODOM AND EGYPT, where also our Lord was crucified." We know that Christ was not crucified in the geographical Sodom or the geographical Egypt. The Passover in Egypt was the antitype of Lot's exodus from Sodom. Lot baked unleavened bread on the night before his escape from Sodom (Genesis 19:3); during the night, intruders attempted to enter Lot's house (Genesis 19:4); Lot was guarded — at the door of his house — by Divine protection (Genesis 19:10). In the same way, the Hebrews baked unleavened bread on the night and before their escape from Egypt; during the night a destroyer attempted to enter the Hebrew's houses; the Hebrews were guarded — at the door of their houses — by Divine protection. Both Sodom and Egypt experienced a rain of fire (Genesis 19:23; Exodus 9:24). "Hebrew" comes from the root that means "to pass over," i.e. into covenant with God. The Divine protection first passed over Lot's threshold in order to protect Lot, as was the case with the Israelites in Egypt. Exodus 12:23 specifically says that God would "pass over the entrance" of the Hebrews' houses so as not to permit "the destroyer to enter your homes"; the destroyer, Satan, was permitted to enter the homes of which God had not passed over their thresholds. So, when it is written that God "smote every firstborn" (Exodus 12:29) because God had specifically said, "I will pass over in the land of Egypt on this night, and I shall strike every firstborn" (Exodus 12:12), those who received such a warning would have understood the more-than-common imagery (at that time) of a King (the "Living God") coming with His executioner, "the one who has the power of death, that is, the devil," (Hebrews 2:14). God did indeed "pass over" Egypt (generally) and He did "pass over" the entrances to the Hebrews' houses (specifically). As God stood at the door to defend the "Hebrews" (those who "passed over" into covenant with God), so Divinity stood at the door to defend Lot from the wickedness of the Sodomites; we may grasp the historical reference: "... their dead bodies will lie in the street of the great city which SPIRITUALLY IS CALLED SODOM AND EGYPT, where also our Lord was crucified," for as the Passover lamb was slain, so Christ is the Lamb Who was slain (Revelation 5:6). Satan must have been already known by Moses to be the slayer of the firstborn (Adam's firstborn) since Moses composed the Torah and since Hebrews 11:28 indeed identifies Satan, not God, as this destroyer of the firstborn: "By faith he [Moses] kept the Passover and the sprinkling of blood, lest HE WHO DESTROYED THE FIRSTBORN should touch them." How could it be believed that Moses *kept* God's command in order to *prevent* God from doing something *according* to God's command? — for this produces a contradiction. Therefore, we can understand why it is written that, "For the Lord will pass through to smite the Egyptians; and when He sees the blood upon the lintel, and on the two side posts, the Lord will PASS OVER THE DOOR, and will not suffer THE DESTROYER to come into your houses to smite you," (Exodus 12:23). Of course, God was not the "Destroyer" (Satan); God was the Defender. Satan is but the executioner, for God is King. As Satan murdered through the "blood" of the grape in Eden, so Satan was prevented from murdering by the blood of a lamb, as he is prevented by the Blood of the "True Vine," the "Lamb" Who is Christ. When we reflect on the imagery of a Warrior-King with

His arms raised up to the height of a bloody lintel on the first Passover, we may understand that, on Passover, Christ had His arms raised up to the height of a bloody lintel and "disarmed the rulers and authorities and made a public example of them, triumphing over them in it" (Colossians 2:15).

In I Corinthians 9, the Apostle Paul argued that those who labor in deciphering and teaching Scripture should be financially supported by the Church so that the laborers may continue in their work, and he made this point through the quotation, "You shall not muzzle an שׁור ox בדישׁו *while it treads* out the grain," (Deuteronomy 25:4). The word שׁור ox has a synonym: אלוּף ox. This synonym אלוּף ox comes from the root אלף *to learn*, and it is used to mean *to teach*. The root דישׁ / דושׁ *to tread, to thresh* has a synonymous root דרשׁ that can mean *to tread* (Amos 5:5), *to seek* (Genesis 25:22), and *to study* (Ecclesiastes 1:13). The Apostle Paul was not making a metaphorical application that artificially utilized the Torah's teaching to substantiate his personal claims; rather, the Apostle Paul wrote according to strict Hebrew diction and made his point by etymological references to synonymous linguistic roots that would have been received with greater ease in his time than in our time. Therefore, when the Torah restricted one from "muzzling an *ox while it treads*," the synonym אלוּף ox is understood regarding the labor of *learning* and *teaching*, and so the "ox," in this case, signified one who labors in the Scriptures for the sake of others; the synonym דרשׁ *to tread* is understood regarding the actual study of the Scriptures, and so, in this case, the "treading" was "studying." The "ox" is the laborer in the Scriptures, and the "treading" signifies his studies — not by simple metaphor, but by precise linguistics through reference to the Torah. The אלוּף ox is also rendered a *guide* (Proverbs 2:17), a *governor* (Zechariah 12:5), a *captain* (Jeremiah 13:21), and *a chief friend* (Proverbs 16:28). Furthermore, the originally quoted word שׁוֹר ox is spelled similarly to the root שׁוּר to *travel*, from where the word שׂרה *traveling company, caravan* is derived:

> "Am I not an APOSTLE [*a guide*] ? Am I not free? Have I not seen Jesus Christ our Lord? Are you not my work in the Lord? If I am not AN APOSTLE TO OTHERS [*a chief friend*], yet doubtless I am to you. For you are the seal of my APOSTLESHIP [*governorship*] in the Lord. My defense to those who examine me is this: Do we have no right to eat and drink? Do we have no right TO TAKE ALONG A BELIEVING WIFE [*traveling company*], as do also the other apostles, the brothers of the Lord, and Cephas? Or is it only Barnabas and I who have no right to refrain from working? Who ever goes to war at his own expense? Who plants a vineyard and does not eat of its fruit? Or who tends a flock and does not drink of the milk of the flock? Do I say these things as a mere man? Or does not the law say the same also? For it is written in the Law of Moses, 'You shall not muzzle an OX WHILE IT TREADS OUT the grain.' Is it OXEN God is concerned about? Or does He say it altogether for our sakes? For our sakes, no doubt, this is written, that he who plows should plow in hope, and he who THRESHES in hope should be partaker of his hope. If we have sown spiritual things for you, is it a great thing if we reap your material things? If others are partakers of this right over you, are we not even more? Nevertheless we have not used this right, but endure all things lest we hinder the gospel of Christ. Do you not know that those who minister the holy things eat of the things of the temple, and those who serve at the altar partake of the offerings of the altar? Even so the Lord has commanded that THOSE WHO PREACH THE GOSPEL should live from the gospel," (I Corinthians 9:1-14).

The *Bible* often employs synonymous ideas and words to refer to the concepts behind another word in order to make a point by the art of riddle-telling; such a methodology highlights critical aspects of an assertion without overtly revealing an allusion.

Since the *Bible* is often treated as but simple, raw history and plain, straight-forward Narrative, it is no wonder that the *Bible* is so often criticized as being contradictory, fallacious, and out-dated, especially when statements are made that claim that the *Bible* fails to discuss important topics like abortion; for such slanderous statements are but based on what would, at first, appear to be the plain meaning of the English Text.

The noun "secel" can mean either "wisdom" or "folly," depending on how it is spelled; thus, "secel" (Ecclesiastes 10:6) and "secel" (Proverbs 12:8) are homophones (words producing identical sounds but differing in orthography). "Secel" spelled "שכל" means "wisdom"; "secel" spelled "סכל" means "folly." The fact that these Hebrew homophones are antonyms (words that have opposite meanings) gives rise to significant wordplay that revolves around Hebrew diction in the Greek New Testament passage of I Corinthians 2:1-14:

> "And I, brethren, when I came to you, did not come with excellence of speech or of WISDOM [secel] declaring to you the testimony of God. For I determined not to know anything among you except Jesus Christ and Him crucified. I was with you in weakness, in fear, and in much trembling. And my speech and my preaching were not with persuasive words of human WISDOM [secel], but in demonstration of the Spirit and of power, that your faith should not be in the WISDOM [secel] of men but in the power of God. However, we speak WISDOM [secel] among those who are mature, yet not the WISDOM [secel] of this age, nor of the

rulers of this age, who are coming to nothing. But we speak the WISDOM [secel] of God in a mystery, the hidden WISDOM [secel] which God ordained before the ages for our glory, which **none of the rulers of this age knew; for had they known, they would not have crucified the Lord of glory**. But as it is written: 'Eye has not seen, nor ear heard, nor have entered into the heart of man the things which God has prepared for those who love Him.' But God has revealed them to us through His Spirit. For the Spirit searches all things, yes, the deep things of God. For what man knows the things of a man except the spirit of the man which is in him? Even so no one knows the things of God except the Spirit of God. Now we have received, not the spirit of the world, but the Spirit who is from God, that we might know the things that have been freely given to us by God. These things we also speak, not in words which man's WISDOM [secel] teaches but which the Holy Spirit teaches, comparing spiritual things with spiritual. But the natural man does not receive the things of the Spirit of God, for they are FOOLISHNESS [secel] to him; nor can he know them, because they are spiritually discerned."

When it was written that "...none of the rulers of this age knew; for had they known, they would not have crucified the Lord of glory..." we might understand that had the people understood who the son of Adam was and that Adam had a son before Cain and Abel (and that the son of Adam was killed accidentally on account of the tree of death), then they would not have killed The Son of Adam on a tree of death. Christ is the "True Vine" (John 15:1) who hung on a tree of death in order to cancel out Satan who was as the false vine who hung on the Tree of Life.

155

Again, Jeremiah 8:8 criticizes the Scribes for having altered the Torah: "How can you say 'We are wise, for we have the Torah of Lord,' when the lying pen of he scribes has handled it falsely?" Such deception, or accident, or both, exists today. The letter שׁ means both a "fire" and a "tooth," and God spoke from on top of the ark, under the wings of the cherubs (Numbers 7:89) where the smoke of the censer covered the atonement cover (Leviticus 16:13); "'Is not My word like a fire?' says the Lord..." (Jeremiah 23:29). Furthermore, the letter "שׁ" is accompanied by a diacritical point on one end or the other; if the dot is placed on top of the right side of this letter שׁ, it makes a "sh" sound, and if the dot is placed on top of the left side of this letter שׂ, it makes an "s" sound. However, the Sacred Text was originally written without vowels or diacritical points. The vowel letters, vowel markings, and diacritical points were, admittedly, placed into the Sacred Text by the Jewish Scribes long after the composition of Scripture. The vocalization of the Torah that is translated into English Bibles reflects the tradition(s) of Judaism, but the unvocalized Torah has nothing to do with Judaism since Judaism did not exist when the Torah was written. Judaism dimly reflects the Torah, but the Torah does not reflect Judaism. It is thought that, perhaps, the "s" sound of words that begin with שׂ was originally produced by the letter ס, but the difficulty with this supposition lies with the word שׂכל *to be wise*; for if this word is uniformly spelled "סכל," it then means exactly the opposite, i.e. *to be foolish*; and to complicate the matter, Ecclesiastes 1:17 uses "שׂכלות" (not סכלות) to mean "folly." When viewing the consonants "שׂכל" (with no vowel markings or diacritical points), they can indicate both *wisdom* (life/ב) and the *opposite of wisdom* (abortion/miscarriage), as in Genesis 3:6. Since the only instance of "שׂכלות" being used to indicate "folly" is found in a work of Solomon (Ecclesiastes 1:17), it can be reasonably pondered that this word (or the ideas behind it) formed part of his prayer to distinguish "טוב *good* לרע *from evil*"

(I Kings 3:9), that is, between *wisdom* and *folly* — especially when considering that Solomon's fatal flaw was that he facilitated the sacrifice of his own son on the Mount of Olives (I Kings 11:7), hence the difference between טוב *beauty* (his foreign wives) and רע *injury* (the sacrifice of his son) or what is commonly referred to as *"good"* and *"evil"* in English... for sacrificing babies was how Molech was worshipped, and this is why Moses smashed the tablets (Acts 7:42-43) and why God intended to kill the worshippers of the golden-calf (Molech) as Stephen stated openly in Acts 7. Genesis 3:6 states,

> "So when the woman saw that THE TREE was good for food, that it was pleasant to the eyes, and a tree desirable to make one wise, she took of its fruit and ate. She also gave to her husband with her, and he ate."

(1) Genesis 3:6 states that "the tree" the woman saw was "good for food"; however, having already observed that the forbidden tree caused vomiting (Job 20) and death (Genesis 3:19), it could not have been "good for food." Having already established that it was seedless, it cannot be attributed to God. Having only two trees with proper names to choose from in this case, the fact that "the tree" was "good for food" necessitates that "the tree" being discussed here was the Tree of Life.

(2) Genesis 3:6 states that "the tree" was "תאוה *enticing* לעינים *to the eyes*"; however, "every tree" that God caused to grow was "נחמד *pleasant* למראה *to the sight*" (Genesis 2:9), not "תאוה *enticing* לעינים *to the eyes*." Having only two trees with proper names to choose from in this case, the fact that "the tree" was "enticing to the eyes" necessitates that "the tree" being discussed here was the Tree of the Knowledge of Good and Evil. One could make the argument that, instead, here we have another example of synonyms. However, that something was a quality of the eyes and not of the sight seems to be

substantiated by Isaiah 11:3 that states "...He shall not judge by what His eyes see..." but rather by His insight.

(3) Genesis 3:6 states that "the tree" was "desirable להשכיל *to make one wise* [from שכל]," but wisdom gives life (Ecclesiastes 7:11-12). Having only two trees, with proper names to choose from in this case, the fact that the forbidden tree caused death necessitates that "the tree" being discussed here was the Tree of Life, especially since Proverbs 3:18 calls "wisdom" a "tree of life." However, the verb that is rendered *to make one wise* can also be read *to bereave one of children; to cause abortion; to miscarry.* It is perceptible that having only two trees with proper names to choose from by the fact that humanity died on account of "the tree" eliminates the possibility of "the tree" having contained "wisdom" since "wisdom" gives "life." That the forbidden tree brought death by way of "folly" necessitates that "the tree" under discussion here is also the Tree of the Knowledge of Good and Evil. In other words, the verb השכיל is to be understood as *to make one wise* AND *to cause miscarriage.* That is, the Tree of Life was both "good for food" and "desirable to make one wise," but the Tree of the Knowledge of Good and Evil was both "enticing to the eyes" and it "caused abortion." Hence, one tree twined by another... the Tree of Life wrapped about by the tree of death, and both must be accounted for here.

Let us consider Deuteronomy 32:32-33:

> "For their VINE is of the VINE of Sodom and of the fields of Gomorrah; their grapes are grapes of gall; their clusters are bitter. THEIR WINE IS THE POISON OF SERPENTS, and the cruel venom of COBRAS";

the reference point is, of course, Eden. Again, some Arabian snakes infect with neurotoxin and one of the effects of such venom is that a victim appears to be drunk, and such a reference was made by King Solomon:

> "Who has DULLNESS OF EYES? — those who stay long at the wine; those who go to seek mixed wine. Do not look at wine when it is red, when it sparkles in the cup and goes down smoothly. At last it BITES LIKE THE SERPENT and STINGS LIKE THE ADDER. Your eyes will see strange things, and your mind utter perverse things. You will be like one who lies down in the midst of the sea, like one who lies on top of a mast [that is, swaying and UNABLE TO KEEP BALANCE]," (Proverbs 23:29-34).

Wine was called the "blood" of the grape (Genesis 49:11; Deuteronomy 32:14). As the blood of the son of Adam ushered death into the world, so The Son of אדם *Man, Adam* brought life through His blood. As Adam and his wife accidentally killed the son of Adam through "eating," so The Son of אדם *Man, Adam* gave us communion. That King Solomon's "wisdom" was a factor at all regarding his righteous judgment over a dead baby (I Kings 3:16-28) and his lack of righteous judgment that killed his infant son (I Kings 11:7) indicates the wordplay around שכל; for since King Solomon was the *wisest* man born of woman (excepting Christ), we can see in him the exact same wordplay that frames the story of "wisdom" in the Eden (the Womb) Narrative regarding a man who was not born of woman — Adam.

To say that "the tree" was "desirable to bereave one of children" would, indeed, sound harsh, and, especially considering that the woman was deceived, "the tree" could not have been "desirable" to cause her to abort her firstborn. Let us reflect on the words "...tree *to be desired* to make one wise..." (Genesis 3:6). The word that is rendered "to be desired" is נחמד and is from the root חמד which can mean "to desire" (in

159

a good sense), or "to covet" (in a bad sense), and the bad sense is employed in the tenth commandment: "You shall not covet thy neighbor's house, you shall not covet thy neighbor's wife..." So, in a good sense, we can comprehend "...tree *to be desired* to make one wise..." and in a bad sense, we can conceive of a covetousness regarding birth. For instance, the rebellious angels of Genesis 6 coveted human women, and having taken them as wives against the design of God, the women bore the Nephilim. The title "Nephilim" is from the root נפל *to fall*, and the noun נפל *untimely birth/abortion/ miscarriage* is derived from this root. II Peter 2:4-5 discusses these rebellious angels and the fallen seed they spread upon the earth:

> "For if God did not spare the angels who sinned, but cast them down to hell and delivered them into chains of darkness, to be reserved for judgment; and did not spare the ancient world, but saved Noah, one of eight people, a preacher of righteousness, bringing in the flood on the world of the ungodly..."

just as Jude 6 states,

> "And the angels who did not keep their proper domain, but left their own abode, He has reserved in everlasting chains under darkness for the judgment of the great day."

We learn from Mark 12:25 that angels were not to marry (and therefore not to have children), and so humanity was given an allowance that the angelic host was not. Satan (who was an angel) coveted (desired) humanity's reproductive capabilities and privileges. Ironically, we read of the "seed" of Satan and the "Seed" of the woman in judgment of Genesis 3. Again, the situation of a vine on a tree was understood as a "wedding."

We have already seen that "trees" are used to describe people in Scripture. Since Christ said that He is "the True Vine" (John 15:1), we may understand the false vine by the "serpent" of Genesis 3 along with a false vine (the forbidden tree). The rebellious angels went against God's design, and their offspring were called the "Fallen Ones," which is derived from a root that yields the word נפל *untimely birth/abortion/ miscarriage*. Accordingly, Satan went against God's design himself, enticed people to do the same, and a miscarriage occurred. The false (forbidden) tree (vine) was enmeshed with a covetousness regarding birth.

The verb השכיל must be read as both *to make one wise* and *to bereave of children*, for the inspired writers of the New Testament must have understood the accounting of more than one definition for words. If we do not understand that the inspired writers knew that the Hebrew diction was not always *this or that* (as Westerners often demand) but rather *this and that*, then we have little evidence to understand Christ's Divinity as it is recorded in Colossians 1. In other words, the first Word of the *Bible* is בראשית *in the beginning*. The word "in" used here is the prefixed particle "ב," the "house," the "womb"; this particle (ב) can mean "in," "with," "by..." The next part of the first Word of Scripture is ראשית *beginning*; this word can mean "beginning," "firstborn," and "first-fruits," and it comes from the root ראש that can mean "head," "chief," "foremost," that is, something or someone exhibiting preeminence. Therefore, the first word in the *Bible* (which is Christ) can be understood in these ways:

> "He is the image of the invisible God, the FIRSTBORN [ראשית] over all creation. For BY HIM all things were created that are in heaven and that are on earth, visible and invisible, whether thrones or dominions or principalities or powers. All things were created through

Him and for Him. And HE IS BEFORE [בראשית] all things, and IN HIM all things consist. And HE IS THE HEAD [ראש] of the body, the church, who is the BEGINNING [ראש], the FIRSTBORN [ראשית] from the dead, that in all things HE MAY HAVE THE PREEMINENCE [ראש]," (Colossians 1:15-20).

In the same way that the Apostle Paul understood that the Hebrew account of Genesis 1-3 was the axis around which the entirety of the Old and New Testaments revolve, and since he wrote the case for Christ's obvious Divinity by utilizing all the definitions of Scripture's first Word, then the only way the Garden of Eden Narrative in Genesis 2-3 makes perfectly consistent sense is to read its words in a similar manner. Let it be stated again: Colossians 1 informs us that Jesus Christ is the First Word of the Hebrew Bible, the word rendered בראשית *in the beginning*; hence, "בראשית *In the beginning* was the WORD, and the WORD [ראשית *Firstborn*] was with God, and the Word was GOD [ראש *Chief*]" (John 1:1), and then, "the WORD was made flesh, and dwelt among us, (and we beheld His glory, the glory as the only BEGOTTEN [ראשית *Firstborn*] of the Father,) full of grace and truth," (John 1:14).

Though the New Testament history occurred after the Old Testament history, the New Testament often serves as a miraculous translation of the vowel-less Torah; the vowel-points are not original, and the vowelized version of the Torah we read in English demands the faulty "Jewish" tradition that simply did not exist when the Torah was written. Thus, we have the veil of the vowels lifted through Christ who fulfilled the entire Torah. As I asked before: Is not the New Testament the living targum of the Old Testament? Surely we cannot think that the New Testament is a mere continuation of raw history, when the Book of Matthew begins by fulfilling the promise made to Abraham based on the prophecy made in the Garden in Eden (Genesis 3:15) regarding the "Seed" further elucidated in Galatians 3:16 through Abraham the Chaldean (Genesis 11:31)... Abraham the Hebrew (Genesis 14:13). If a "Hebrew" inherently indicated a "Jew," then how could Abraham have been a Chaldean Hebrew? The fact that Abraham was both a Hebrew and a Chaldean indicates, yet again, that a "Hebrew" is one who "PASSES OVER" into covenant with God, as is the root of the word "Hebrew": "Understand, then, that those who believe are children of Abraham" (Galatians 3:7), and such a belief is an action for, "...do you want to know, O foolish man, that faith without works is dead? Was not Abraham our father justified by works when he offered Isaac his son on the altar? Do you see that faith was working together with his works, and by works faith was made perfect?" (James 2:20-22). If the Torah was the faith of Judaism, then Judaism would not claim that, by doctrine, one must accuse and reject Jesus, Who died on PASSOVER, in order to accord with the Torah, as it is so taught in the "sacred" text of Judaism, the Babylonian Talmud. The Talmud's "Sanhedrin" does indeed blasphemously say that Jesus practiced "sorcery" and "enticed Israel to apostasy," for this is the doctrine of Rabbinic Judaism (Mark 3:22). Those of the Jewish faith call the Talmud "Law" or "Torah" or "Oral Torah," and this is the same manner of "Law" the Pharisees accused Christ of breeching. That Christ was the King of the Jews is obvious by the fact that He is the King of all Creation since He said that, "All power is given unto Me in heaven and in earth," (Matthew 28:18). For a "Replacement Theologian" to claim that Christians have replaced Jews would only prove consistent if one were to make the mistake of thinking that the Written Torah was somehow "Jewish," which it is not. It seems that both the support of and the opposition to such a supposed "replacement" have argued over a premise that never existed in reality. A similar mistake has been made by arguing about how a deadly tree gave "wisdom," or by arguing over why a loving God would have planted the forbidden tree in the first place, when wisdom gives life and God did not plant the forbidden tree. It is my opinion that Diodorus Siculus was correct when he stated that "...it is by means of speech alone that one man is able to gain ascendancy over the many; and, in general, the impression made by every measure that is proposed corresponds to the power of the speaker who presents it, and we describe great and good men as 'worthy of speech,' as though therein they had won the highest prize of excellence," (*Library of History*, Book I); for such was the case of the Fall in Eden as induced by the double-tongued fiend and as allowed by the first human priest of God.

All vegetation that can be attributed to God yielded "seed," was "good" (generally) and was "good for food" (specifically), was "according to its kind," and was "pleasant to the sight," (Genesis 1:11-13; 2:9). However, the Tree of the Knowledge of Good and Evil could not have been planted by God because it did not bear seed, was not good (generally), was bad for food (specifically), inhibited multiplication, was of unlike kinds, and was not "pleasant to the sight" (Genesis 2:9). God has been falsely accused of creating a conduit that destroyed the creation that He loves, bled for, died for, and rose for... the very creation to which He gave His Holy Word.

Exodus 20:8 says, "זכור *Remember* the day of the Sabbath to sanctify it," and Deuteronomy 5:12 repeats the command by saying, "שמור *Guard* the day of the Sabbath to sanctify it." The word שמר *guard* also means *preserve*, and so as we can preserve something in our memory, we can remember to guard our minds. That is, the word "guard" is the same word used in relation to Adam when Scripture states that the Lord God set the man in the garden to cultivate her ולשמרה *and to guard her* (Genesis 2:15). However, we have noticed that a faithful recount of God's Word did not proceed out of the mouth of the deceived bride, and Adam did not guard the garden or his "garden"... for, by allowing Satan to walk in Eden, Adam allowed Satan to acquire Eden, since the formal act of walking through territory was an action that denoted legal acquisition (which is the reason that Abram was to walk through the land in Genesis 13:17). Consider the shameful filth that walks through people's homes at the click of a buttons... and consider how children are equipped by their parents with personal communication devices that provide even easier access to swift and dark destruction. Imagine if, three thousand years from now, people look back to written records of our time and assume that we used live rodents to navigate our way through computers because we have called such a navigation device a "mouse," and it might prove easier to grasp how a mindset that prefers mass-media to Scripture fervently demands that people believe in talking reptiles. Who then is the "bride" today? Christ remembered and guarded, but have we recounted the story of the Word faithfully?

We all make many mistakes, and I pray that both God and man forgive me if I have committed any blunders or oversights within this small work of mine that is written for the advancement of God's kingdom. At the same time, let us observe that by overlooking the deliberate descriptions laid down for us in the Text, many otherwise rational people have been held under the bondage of believing in ridiculous fairytales out of righteous fear of damnation, and the same bondage has often driven rationally-thinking people away from the modern Church. Today, given the choice between (1) the blasphemous stupidity displayed on glowing screens and (2) the pure wisdom displayed in God's Holy Word, it seems as if it is still man's nature to abuse the gift of choice by consistently proving himself to be a wretch. The impossible and contradictory fable-version of Eden has dominated *Bible*-study for far too long, though it was not part of the early

Church. Many would-be believers have mocked Christians because the very first story of humanity seems, to them, to be little more than mythological fancy riddled with contradictions and poor editing that was written during some remote era devoid of true learning — when, in fact, the very first story of humanity concerns "wisdom" itself, and it revolves around the wordplay of the word השכיל *to make one wise.*

Let it be understood clearly that God did not plant the forbidden tree, and I repent for ever having accused Him of doing so.

Glory Be to God Almighty!

NOTES

Note 1 (pages 22, 137)

It cannot be that "Ethiopia" is meant by "Cush" regarding Eden and the four rivers. Either there were "Cushites" other than Ethiopians (as some scholars believe), or כוש = "Cush" was read (and so pointed) in the Massoretic Text instead of something like כוס = "Cose" (כוס). Dr. Bullinger noted,

> "Eden. In the cuneiform texts = the plain of Babylonia, known in the Accado-Sumerian as edin = 'the fertile plain,' called by its inhabitants Edinu," (*Companion Bible*, Bullinger; p. 5); 'Gihon' = the river E. of the Tigris. The modern Kerkhah, and ancient Khoaspes, rising in the mountains of the Kassi. Kas has been confused with the Heb. Cush. It is not the African Cush or Ethiopia, but the Acadian Kas," (*Companion Bible, Bullinger*; p. 6)

Dr. Bullinger's assessment may indeed be correct. At the same time, I suspect that the word rendered "Cush" in our *Bibles* today once formed a wordplay around the feminine noun "cose," that is כוס *cup*, which is from the root *to cover, to hide*. Concave vessels were once used to symbolize wombs, perhaps because one's reflection in a concave basin is upside-down as a baby is so situated in the womb. Similarly, the convection of a hill or mountain was also understood to symbolize a womb.

Again, we understand that a tree of light is a tree of life, for the Scriptures continually interchange "light" and "life" or use "light" to parallel "life." We understand that the menorah is a tree of light. Therefore, a tree of light is a tree of life, which helps to explain why, when regarding idiomatic usages of words in Scripture, it is apparent that the expression, "To give him always a LIGHT" (II Kings 8:19) means "to give him an HEIR to sit on his throne," and why the expression, "Thou wilt light my candle (Psalm 18:28) means "He will give me light and happiness; He will give me an HEIR." Since we have already seen that "wisdom," "light," and "life" are held in parallel, it is no wonder that Ecclesiastes 7:11-12 states that "wisdom" gives "life." Furthermore, since we have understood the indications of "seed," "fruit," in relation to "progeny," it is no wonder that the Hebrew letter "ב" (which is the Hebrew number "2") is understood as both a "house" and "wisdom." The name of the letter ב is בית *a house*. A woman (generally) and a womb (specifically) are referred to as a "house" in Scripture, which is a reason why it is written that God "built" (ויבן) the woman in Genesis 2:22, like a man "builds" a house. The ancient Jews used to teach their children the alphabet by referring to the letter ב as "wisdom."

A "cup," a "bowl," and a "threshold" were all held synonymously in reference to the womb (and therefore the opening to it). For instance, the word "בטן" is rendered (1) *bowl* in I Kings 7:20, (2) *belly* in Numbers 5:22, and (3) *womb* in Genesis 25:23; and knowing that a "door" was a reference to a "womb" (Job 3:10, Song of Songs 8:9), the "basin" of a door is the same as its threshold, for such is the סף *basin or threshold* that was used to hold the blood of the Passover in Exodus, and we may observe the *Babylonian Talmud's* "Megillah," where it refers to women as "vessels." Let us recall that Song of Songs 7:3 refers to a woman's navel as a אגן *goblet*, a *cup*, and consider how offspring is compared to האגנות *the bowls* in Isaiah 22:24, for the words *cup* and *bowl* are one and the same. Since we know that a basin and a cup function in the same way (and are, in some cases, the same word), we must take into consideration the menorah's cups (Exodus 25:31-32). The menorah's גביעים *cups* come from the root גבע *to be high,* and the word *hill* is derived from this root as well; however, its synonym "cose" כוס *cup* is from the root *to cover, to hide.* A cup and a בטן *bowl (belly, womb)* function similarly. So, a "cup" can be understood גבע to *be high* or כוס *to be covered*, depending on which synonym is employed. Figuratively regarding the "light," Christ said,

> "You are the LIGHT of the world. A city on a HILL cannot be HIDDEN. Neither do people light a LAMP and put it under a BOWL [i.e. *to be covered*]. Instead they PUT IT ON ITS STAND [i.e. *to be high*], and it gives LIGHT to everyone in the HOUSE. In the same way, let your light shine before men, that they may see your good deeds and praise your Father in heaven," (Matthew 5:14-16).

Turning back to the rivers in relation to "Cush" and Eden (the Womb), we may note that the river *Gihon* (which means *Bringing Forth, especially of a pregnant woman*) is the *second* river, and the number "2" in Hebrew is the letter ב, the *house*, and, I think, this river flowed around the whole land of Cose (not "Cush"); that is, the land that is "covered" like a "cup" (a womb):

"Now a river went out of Eden to water the garden, and from there it parted and became four riverheads. The name of the first is פישון *Diffusion of Waters*; it is the one which skirts the whole land of חוילה *Bringing Forth, especially of a pregnant woman*, where there is gold. And the gold of that land is good. Bdellium and the onyx stone are there. THE NAME OF THE SECOND RIVER IS גיחון *Belly, as the Source of the Fetus*; IT IS THE ONE WHICH GOES AROUND THE WHOLE LAND OF CUSH [*cose* = THE COVERED CUP = **THE WOMB** (?)]. The name of the third river is חדקל *Light, Swift*; it is the one which goes toward the east of אשור *Lifted Up, Exalted*. The fourth river is the פרת *Fruitful*," (Genesis 2:10-14).

The main reason why I believe the word that is now rendered "Cush" to have been originally a wordplay on "cup" in the passage above is that "cose" or כוס *cup* is from the root *to cover, to hide*, in opposition to the "cup" that comes from the root גבע *to be high* — for the very next river "... is the one which goes toward the east of אשור *Lifted Up, Exalted*." So, understanding that an "heir" and a "light" are synonymous and that Ecclesiastes 8:1 indicates that the result of "wisdom" is "light," on top of the fact that "wisdom" and "womb" are linked to the number "2," which is the letter ב, the *house*, it would again seem as if Christ made reference to this SECOND river when He said,

"You are the LIGHT of the world. A city on a **HILL** cannot be **HIDDEN**. Neither do people light a LAMP and put it under a BOWL [i.e. *to be covered*]. Instead they PUT IT ON ITS STAND [i.e. *to be high*], and it gives LIGHT to everyone in the HOUSE. In the same way, let your light shine before men, that they may see your good deeds and praise your Father in heaven," (Matthew 5:14-16);

for one "cup" (womb) is **hidden**, and another "cup" (womb) is **lifted up**. If the "Sh" letter ש in the word "Cush" was originally read as "S," then the word Cush could read כוס *Cose*, the womb, the hidden כוס *cup*, the SECOND land regarding the SECOND river; and since 2 = ב = *the womb*, it would stand to reason that the river associated with it in the Text was the river גיחון *Belly, as the Source of the Fetus*.

Accordingly, knowing that a CUP can indicate something lifted up (like a HILL or mountain) or something COVERED (like that which is hidden), the conclusion stated above would say much to Christ identifying Himself as The Son of Adam when He stated,

"Daughters of Jerusalem, weep not for me, but weep for yourselves, and for your children. For, behold, the days are coming, in the which they shall say, 'Blessed are the BARREN, and the WOMBS that never bare, and the paps which never gave suck.' Then shall they begin to say to the MOUNTAINS [i.e. *to be high*], 'Fall on us'; and to the HILLS, '**COVER US** [כסונו]...' [Hosea 10:8]," (Luke 23:28-31).

Furthermore, that "hills" and "mountains" are even discussed in this context points to the Hebrew peculiarity of the words "mountain" and "to become pregnant" which sound very similar to each other. Such Hebrew wordplay is employed in Galatians 4:24 regarding a mountain and a pregnancy, for the pattern of pregnancy was recorded on Mt. Sinai (see note 7).

The knowledge that a womb was considered a "bowl" and a "cup" sheds much light on the wordplay of this passage:

> "If a man begets a hundred children and lives many years, so that the days of his years are many, but his soul is not satisfied with goodness, or indeed he has no burial, I say that A STILLBORN CHILD is better than he — for it comes in vanity and departs in darkness, and ITS NAME IS COVERED [יכסה] with darkness," (Ecclesiastes 6:3-4).

Note 2 (page 53)

Regarding the ruinous mixture of unlike entities, let us not fall into the trap of considering races to be "unlike" when it is obviously a broader likeness that is being discussed; for Moses married a woman of a different race than himself. When Moses' sister complained about the union of Moses' light skin with his wife's dark skin, God punished Moses' sister with skin that was as "white as snow" with leprosy (Numbers 12:10); the punishment fit the offense perfectly.

Note 3 (page 60)

For a more detailed description of gardens and paradises, see the book *The Knowledge of Good and Evil*, by Joshua Collins.

Note 4 (page 65)

As far as the Tree of Life being a tree of "light," and therefore "wisdom," I do not believe that the olive-tree is intended here (at least not exclusively), but rather the fig-tree (at least inclusively). That is, Revelation 22:2 states that the Tree of Life produces 12 kinds of fruit, so (at least by way of astronomical imagery) this tree could not be exclusively of the fig; yet, it would seem that of the 12 kinds of fruit, the fig is the most illustrative for the history in Genesis 2-3 since the subject under great stress is birth. Revelation 22:2 states specifically that the leaves of the Tree of Life are for "healing," and we find the parallel to such healing in the story of King Hezekiah (II Kings 20): Hezekiah suffered from a malignant boil, and Isaiah (through God's power and provision) healed the boil with "a lump of figs," (II Kings 20:7). After Hezekiah's blunder in II Kings 20:12-15, Isaiah told Hezekiah, "Some of your own sons who are born to you shall be taken away," (II Kings 20:18). Since the letters בכורה can mean *the early fig*, the *firstling* of a man, and *birthright*, it would stand to reason that as the poisonous vine-tree (the forbidden tree) coiled about the fig tree (the Tree of Life), so the serpent extinguished man's firstborn in order to usurp the birthright. Consider Christ wrapped in burial clothes in a manger, an ark. That Adam and his wife covered their loins with fig-leaves would then have indicated that they were attempting to heal their loins due to the death that had passed through the woman's door during the usurpation of the birthright by the death of their firstborn. Perhaps the imagery with which we are dealing illustrates that the fig is but one of the 12 "fruits" of the tree. Whichever way, the birthright is among the major issues here, and according to what I can derive from diction, the early fig seems fitting. I am more than open to better suggestions.

Note 5 (page 85)

Plato used the same figure when he reworked the Aposiopesis of Genesis 3:22 into the last line of his Atlantis tale, which can be found at the conclusion of his book *Critias*.

Note 6 (page 130)

Consider:

"Then one of them, which was a lawyer, asked Him a question, tempting Him, and saying, 'Master, which is the great commandment in the Torah?' Jesus said unto him, *'Thou shalt love the Lord thy God with all thy heart, and with all thy soul, and with all thy mind* [Deuteronomy 6:5]. This is the first and great commandment. And the second is like unto it, *Thou shalt love thy neighbor as thyself* [Leviticus 19:18]. On these two command-ments hang all the law and the prophets,'" (Matthew 22:35-40).

Notice that Christ's commands are Torah laws. Since we know that Ephesians 2 states that the Torah is the "enmity" discussed in Genesis 3:15, then we understand why I Timothy 1:9 states that the Torah is not made for the righteous, but for the wicked; for the Torah is a guide to insure that if one does not love God and man, one will be compelled to act in, at least, a pretended accordance with God and man under penalty of punishment. Hence, it was the pretended accordance with God and man that the Pharisees practiced — which is why they made up their own laws (The Oral Law) and passed them off, falsely, as God's laws, even though their Oral Law contradicted the Torah. Their acts were examples of hypocrisy, and their supposed "love" of God and man was feigned; this is why they thought that works could save them, for they placed raw works above the righteous motivation necessary to do those very same works properly. The Torah's aim (made for the wicked) was the heart, for if one's heart and mind (same word in Hebrew) were oriented towards Heaven, then one's actions would by nature follow one's heart, thus making one's works an outward manifestation of one's internal state... and this process was inverted by the Pharisees. One, quick reading of the *Bible* illustrates that good works alone are insufficient regarding salvation (II Timothy 1:9); however, we are commanded to do good works (II Timothy 3:17), and such works should be exacted as manifestations of inward convictions spurred by faith in Christ. The entirety of the Book of James illustrates what belief and faith truly are, and there is no such thing as "faith" without works by which faith is illustrated. So, when Christ discussed the "love" for God and man, I John illustrates such a "love" when it says,

> "My little children, let us not love in word, neither in tongue; but IN DEED and in truth," (I John 3:18).

> "By this we know that we love the children of God, when we love God, AND KEEP HIS COMMANDMENTS. For this is the love of God, that WE KEEP HIS COMMANDMENTS: and his commandments are not grievous," (I John 5:2-3).

So, the *legality* of the matter is a product of the heart, but the state of one working with one's hands only (in place of working genuinely) is the state of those for whom the Torah was written: the wicked (I Timothy 1:9). Abraham is a key figure in the writings of Paul because Abraham followed the Torah before it was given to Moses (Genesis 26:5) on account of his faith, for Abraham DID all that God told him to do with a loving heart for God. Righteous acts should display the faith that precedes them. Since dietary regulations (excepting the prohibition against the forbidden tree) only came after the giving of the Torah to Moses, we understand why, like Abraham, we are not restricted to such regulations, as is illustrated thoroughly in Romans and Galatians. We must feed on the Word of God. We must *act*, that is, we must *bear fruit*. Keep in mind that Sodom and Gomorrah were destroyed in the days of Abraham, before Moses received the Torah.

Note 7 (pages 110, 146)

The science concealed beneath the Torah is ב *wisdom*, that is, the inner workings of the *womb*. In other words, the knowledge that is concealed beneath the surface of the Torah is the knowledge of human gestation (wisdom/womb), which is why the first story of man deals with an innocent person (the son of Adam) who was slain due to his parents' rebellion and subsequent ignorance, as was mirrored with the Pharisees and Sadducees in their rebellion and subsequent ignorance regarding the death of Christ. As such, the seven feasts of the Torah are set to mirror human gestation, and this is a reason why "wisdom" (the womb/ the house) is such an emphatic topic at the beginning and the conclusion of the Torah; the Torah is framed by ב = *wisdom* = *the womb* = *the house* = *the temple of God*. Since the entire Torah concealed the knowledge of human development in the womb, **we have here infallible proof of the Divine Inspiration of Scripture** because no human being during the days of Moses had any knowledge as to the stages of gestation through science; the cameras doctors use to take pictures within the womb had not yet been invented. No one could have known how a human is formed in the womb through science while Scripture was being penned, even though the Torah itself reflected how a child is so formed.

> "As thou KNOWEST NOT what is the way of the spirit, NOR HOW THE BONES DO GROW IN THE WOMB of her that is with child:
> even so thou knowest not the works of God who maketh all,"
> (Ecclesiastes 11:5).

The only One Who could have known how infants grow in the womb was the Architect Himself, God Almighty, the One Who came down and worked as a Carpenter. It was His Spirit Who dictated Scripture, and it was the Architect's Spirit who gave the blue-print necessary to build the house (the temple, the womb, the wisdom). Since the Torah is imbued with the blue-print of life itself — the very plans to build the house (the womb) — we can understand that, as no such knowledge had yet reached man through science, a Child was to be born according to the plan of the Torah; this

Child was Christ, the "Seed" discussed in Genesis 3:15, for

> "...before faith came, we were kept under the Torah, shut up unto the faith which should AFTERWARDS BE REVEALED. Wherefore the Torah was our SCHOOLMASTER TO BRING US UNTO CHRIST, that we might be justified by faith," (Galatians 3:23-24).

Humanity did not know how the processes of the womb worked when the Torah was first penned, but in exacting the will of God through the Torah, people were to work in such a way that the reason for the design of the Torah would be revealed in due time — when Christ came to earth. Such revelation was not revealed to the Jewish elites who changed the official celebration of the new year to be in autumn when, in fact, the Torah's new year (Exodus 12:2) is in the spring, the "time of life" (Genesis 18:14). By altering the "beginning" of the year, the Jews during the earthly days of Christ were guilty of putting death into life (celebrating the time of death as the "time of life"). Accordingly, we can understand why the Apostle Paul called the Torah (that concealed the processes of the womb) the "Ministry of Death" in II Corinthians 3:7 in reflection of the ABORTION in the WOMB, i.e. the DEATH in EDEN; consider that The Son of Man was put to death (in "the time of life") for doing no wrong, as is the case of the slain infants when abortion is committed, for we must at all times keep in the forefront of our minds that the Torah counts the festival days from **conception**, not from birth. Those who were instructed in the ancient physiology and in the art of riddles were not taught the reasons of things, but were rather students of the well-cultivated art of concealing knowledge beneath the surface of what at first seems to be a fantastic tale that was particularly veiled from the commoner who lacked devotion in his/her study. In other words, and in our context, it was once expected that those who did not deliberately seek the answers to riddles would only be left with stories that seemed impossible, and under such a supposition was Scripture written. The Hebrew word דרש to *seek* also means *to study* and *to tread*. Let us walk with God.

Final Thoughts

Having been taught many errant things concerning "divine revelation" from my youth upwards, once I decided to follow Christ at the age of 18, I also taught others what I was taught in my best efforts to glorify God. I continued in my error so greatly that I published many faulty things in my first book called *The Order of Creation*. I have found that what is CALLED "divine revelation" by many in the "Church" often collides with Scripture disastrously. Once I discovered many of my ridiculous errors, I blushed myself into the removal of my very first book from print so as not to mislead others as I myself had been mislead; consider my shame in the fact that I primarily wrote this book for a new convert... I ask forgiveness from God and man. I only did what I thought was "obedient" and "reverent." I hope God, man, and this particular proselyte accept the book you are reading in place of *The Order of Creation.* I am beyond thankful to be, at the very least, pointed towards a more accurate direction, though I have a long way to go in overcoming the many deficiencies of my mortality.

Thank you.

Joshua Collins

DID GOD PLANT THE FORBIDDEN TREE?

ISBN 978-1-935434-42-9

Post Gutenberg Books™

an imprint of
GlobalEd AdvancePress

www.ingramcontent.com/pod-product-compliance
Lightning Source LLC
Chambersburg PA
CBHW070800100426
42742CB00012B/2202